# DEATH

*poems by Gordon Massman*

**N꜀Y Books**™

The New York Quarterly Foundation, Inc.
New York, New York

NYQ Books™ is an imprint of The New York Quarterly Foundation, Inc.

The New York Quarterly Foundation, Inc.
P. O. Box 2015
Old Chelsea Station
New York, NY 10113

www.nyq.org

First Edition

Layout and Design by Jessica S. Eichman | www.glasseggdesign.com
Cover Design by Noah Saterstrom | www.noahsaterstrom.com

Library of Congress Control Number: 2014933705

ISBN: 978-1-935520-97-9
ISBN for set: 978-1-935520-98-6

There is almost nothing bad that I couldn't say about humans and humankind. And yet my pride in them is so great that there is only one thing I really hate: their enemy, death.

—Elias Canetti

# PROLOGUE

**D**EATH IS slick-hair comedian entering klieg light, falling on face, drunk

Death is clown on tiny bike, plastic hair, daisy water pistol, knees wedging
     chest, flies down ramp, flips, spins, lands beyond bucket in elephant shit

Death is Clem Kadiddlehopper plastered by exploding coal furnace

Death is Michigan J. Frog excavated from crypt bellowing *Hello My Baby*

Death is pioneer aviator at bottom of cliff wadded in wings

Death is Costello touching Mummy over shoulder stuttering "AAAAAbbbbott!
     AAAAAAbbbbbott!"

Death is homemade rocket corkscrewing off pad, careening downward, igniting
     pine needles

Death avoiding ladder smashes into mirror

Pie creams Death dodging pie

Death in tree saws victim off limb, tree crashes down

At last second matador whips cape from charging Death which smashes into
     anvil

Poking shotgun down wabbit hole barrel pokes up another which blows off
     Death's ass

Death crushes buttercup on Ferdinand's nose sensitizing him to nature's excru-
     ciation

Death flings milk across night sky hungering all breasts into perpetuity

Death fuses lovers together like smashed cars

Death dances Egyptian, Bristol, black bottom buzz; stomp, mashed potato, bony
    maronie; loco-motion, shag, razzamatazz; Freddie, flapper, old soft shoe
    before a jam-packed judiciary, sheepishly grinning

Death is Little Ricky whipping trap set into a mouth froth

Death is Cheetah apoplectically screeching beside Tarzan slammed unconscious
    into a tree

Death hammers eyes into a book, removes them long enough to hammer them
    into another

Death between teeth grinds, mashes, tosses, beats enzyme-saturated beef, strings
    it in waves to lung-blood exchange deep in gut only to snatch another in
    greed's eternal combustion machine

Death is spark which commands hands to pound petroglyphs into rock, not the
    message itself but impetus which seizes hands to strike into perpetuity
    whorls of self's irrepressible heart-print

Death is eyeball of ox, human, monkey, rat, all world's perceiving eyeballs
    dumped into a drum, tumble-turned such that they catching each other
    inverted sideways slantways backward in slices and flashes are rolled upon
    a field of fertility or desolation to stare forever at what they stop upon

Death is what fixes boot heel in root-system, secures weapon to gut, squeezes
    trigger, shreds trees, animals, villages, children, and what impels hot cas-
    ings to pour out helicopters like water

Death is what grinds mustard seed with pestle, husks corn, threshes rye, slaugh-
    ters cattle, shells nuts, gins cotton, pasteurizes milk, systematizes barter,

establishes economies, installs governments, creates declarations, manifestos, ideologies, mythologies, liberation theologies and missionaries armed with M-1s, M-60s, M-3 Grease Guns, Ithaca 37s, Claymore M18-A21s, white phosphorous, fragmentation grenades, flamethrowers, M-20 recoilless, napalm, agent orange, 75mm pack howitzers, daisy cutters, F111 aardvarks, UH-1 Huey and LARCS amphibious vehicles affixed with swinging crucifix to spread the word

Death is engine of ambition colliding with engine of achievement, hunger colliding with labor, ardor with lover, revenge with victim, when engine of virtuosity collides with scalpel, aesthetics with epiphany, politics with extermination

Death is the farthest one can go before slamming into the wall enclosing infinity

Death is spit breaking down calories in catalytic jet empowering brain to perceive the threat, and body with the stamina to engage it

Death is just, just, just a baked potato melting butter

Death, aching with egotism, makes her come so hard her groan gushes out chimney, bells through sky, folds backward like momentous biblical lips, swallows the world

# PART I

*E*AT CHUNKY MONKEY in opposition to death.

In opposition to death, email congress a photocopy of feet.

Oppose death by kissing goat bristles.

Oppose death in Synagogue storage closet.

In opposition to death confess sin through cheese grater.

In opposition to death burst through smoke straddling a rocket.

Oppose oblivion by marrying a lizard.

Oppose extirpation without a condom.

In opposition to death lick beads off flagon of etiquette.

In contradiction to necrosis calculate specific gravity of zero; plant a
tulip bulb upside-down, stand in earth inverted against it, feel it
twist toward the core.

In opposition to death pen the dictionary of immortal phrases uttered
by the rat-tailed possum.

In contradistinction to extermination suck gorilla glue, ballpoint pen
ink, tube of cobalt blue psychological wreckage, count to twenty,
burst into the Funky Chicken.

Countermand eternal peace & dear departure by issuing gutturals,
finger-blubbering lips.

Extradite oblivion by standing trial for promiscuity before the Supreme
Court of McConigel's Mucky Duck.

Stuff love missives inside gnocchi, load on spoon, catapult into the face
of surcease, to wit: spit.

In contraindication to eradication douse molasses over nut, bury to
neck in jungle muck, without indignation feel queen creep down
neck to squirt in gut innumerable eggs of spectacular derision.

In opposition to death maintain tortoise in marriage bed, prop on giant
bivalve shell your two crushable precious heads.

Crawl inside, against *homo-interrptus*, pine tree's crisp clean yellow
splinters the instant it cracks from logger's saw anointing yourself
with sap, resin, purity, prayer.

Against decomposition ride flagellating silt-cloud crocodile to the
tumor of rage at the center of nothingness.

Let there be hair, gelatin, spleen, secretion.

In antithesis to rictus have sex, men, with tuba; women with clarinet.

Oppose death by forming an ice-brick of mine tailings, nuclear waste, industrial sludge, raw sewage, culm dump, leach pool, industrial run-off, hypoxia bloom, and The Pacific Trash Vortex and melt it over the genitals of your vilest enemy—in my case the collective genitalia of the captains of mediocrity.

Highlight in yellow the Pope's underwear to interdict demise.

Intercede against derailment atop a clot of dead monsters.

To oppose death, I say, crane neck toward mama, receive worm of bitterness.

Let there be heart bedlam,

Brain turmoil,

Leg chaos,

Tangle of fingers,

Infelicity tongue,

Concussing ear drum,

Jocularity thumb,

Root bound skull,

Dish stack disk,

Bony Maronie hips,

Tropical Achilles,

Riotous lips,

Foamy ocean blood,

And a neck like Vesuvius.

Sometimes I have such fits of happiness I could scream.

*P*ROMISE ME you'll take care of Edward.

Course, Rick says.

Love you.

Love you, too.

Rick suddenly realizes what he's accepted. Edward's impossible.

Years perhaps.

It's a paycheck.

Perhaps it won't be horrible.

Mother looks like she's not terminal.

She's cranked to sitting. Chattering. Eating. Cracking jokes.

She wants ice cream.

Daddy's absent depending on exhaustion.

Rick takes him home.

Shoreline to Doddridge to Santa Fe to Barracuda to Miramar Place

Which swallows him in history.

He poops his diapers.

His pants fall down.

He can't work buttons.

Brown carpet stains.

Rick disinfects.

Daddy eats Rick's meat loaf, potatoes.

He's still got teeth.

Then back to hospital.

Who's sick?

Oh yes, Roslyne.

Dementia would lash him fiendishly

But for Rick

Who shores him up.

You didn't need to come, she admonishes Daddy,

Code for "go away".

Our vigil relieved

My sister and I go for supper.

Crab cakes.

We reminisce.

Nana. Papa. Lynne. Andee. Port Aransas.

Wasn't all awful.
For all her locked sprockets and cogs my sister sobs.
I don't know.
I never knew anything.
I operate in brilliant egotistical blindness.
I remember how cancer beautified a friend,
Thinning him to luminosity
Before execution.
Mother looks ravaged by influenza.
My sister greases mother's lips,
Unkinks hair.
Daddy accuses her of fakery.
Wanders down corridor.
Night. All go to bed
Doubtlessly wrapped in trepidation.
My dreams plaster,
Freaky dislocations.
Flashlight Daddy ghosts the house.
Blackout curtains.
Morning. Breakfast.
Daddy slurps Coco Puffs.
Muffin crunches twigs and sticks.
I mash instant oats.
Pink Formica table top.
Burglar-proof iron window-bars.
Brass wall clock.
Museum of 50s.
Heavy tropical air.
Miramar to Central to Shoreline Drive to hospital.
I drop Muffin and Daddy at entrance.
Park in structure.
Meet in lobby.
Sometimes it hits us unawares.
Press button 6.
We swing abreast like a door into her room.
Slats agape, tray at waist, Mother motored upright, beaming.

*I* BREATHE NAPALM, bathe in agent orange
Syphilis eats my brain
I walk in typhoid woven socks, tie malarial shoes
I drink drafts of diphtheria-beer
And scrofula-fortified port
I dance smallpox foxtrot
drool on tetanus sheet
I wash clothes in gangrene suds
Dry in dysentery air
I drive a pulled hand grenade
Rock in frag bomb chair
Booby traps stud my lover's sex
I pulse out cluster bombs
Let it be known botany threads
Smallpox through my eyes,
Zoology nerve gas
Through nose
I eschew biochemical labs
And avoid slaughter of war
I deny paranoia of conspiracy freaks
And escape dejection
Of street
Species homo sapiens—
Every genius, fool—
Is indestructible
Cannot die
And its cells refuse to retreat
From trichinosis of the crucifix
And botulism of the star.

*H*OW LUCKY for Christ he didn't die when crucified.
Who wouldn't wish same fantastic fate.
God-immortality.
Pancreatic cancer triumphs: Bingo! Resurrection!
Myocardial thrombosis: Bang! Resuscitation.
What bull doesn't want eternal stomp,
Immemorial rutty mischief?
I would gorge debauched, expire of petrification, rise to romp again,
Dissolute.
What fiendish bliss to run amok, slamming grillwork through vendor cart,
    sparking guardrail, and, decapitated, projectile discharge out convertible
Only to resurrect, reaffix noggin, hitch knickers
And walk.
Jollity. *Jingle Bells, Jingle Bells.*
Libertine doing the Loosey Goosey
In a sleazy nightclub flinging sweat like a bedlamite.
Greased and frigid cardiac arrest
On a slimy floor
And arisen wearing a parrot shirt
Praising hedonism.
Only one mortal, Jesus, becomes Superman
Leaving the rest in gutter, impotent.
Bob at factory.
Jack with listings.
Karen at cubicle.
Commissions. Presentations.
Superman dribbles pity-spittle.
Who wouldn't want time to stop,
Freeing the living from deterioration, freezing the unborn child from Birth,
Like a world under glass,
Forever unchanging, incorruptible.
What a riveting fantasy,
Christmas Eve, 2012.

Absently, I take a pen, doodle ridiculous
Stick figure image
Fantasizing omnipotence as I die.

# *D*ECEMBER 31, 2012

Dear Dad,

Rage bursts through your lips like a second face, beast slithers poisonously from hers. Warring creatures in each other's clasp, flipping, crashing: you and mom chilling my spine. I, busted-out hostage, flew on wax paper down slide to crack cocaine, cuff unraveled, derelict, felon, my comfort and friend. By drugs I die. We failed each other, you by wrecking my childhood, I by continued wrecking. Neither doctor nor lawyer but splinter in eye. I fucked up. I'm zero. A hepatitis C, bench warrant, half-way house junkie. I'm your scofflaw looting Family Dollar, turning tricks for rocks. Here's my syllogism: I love cocaine. Cocaine is death. Ergo, I love death. You don't love me, I don't love you. You love poetry, I love highs. Death accompanies us differently. One day, inconveniencing ambition, you'll get the nod. An occasion ripe to summarize: were you to level "egotist," "sociopath," "ingrate," "fool," "coward," "trash," you would be justified. This is the stuff of psycho-physiological destruction. We are both already reasonably dead.

Merry Christmas,
Kenneth

*I*LACKED COURAGE to murder mother and now that she's dying
Am devastated.

She stretches before me, rictal, almost apologetic.
She appreciates my predisposition.

Time now squeezes her. My ineptitude infuriates.
This natural causes business—

Catheter, diaper, drip tube, lousy food—
Honors nobody.

I planned her murder in '62 but collapsed on sand
In quivering jelly-mass.

Now I sit bed-side like floor bulge,
Mockery to my shoes.

Death's clumsiness humiliates the living; most murders go
Uncommitted. I love her.

Son-love laces mother like blood laces sputum.
Love without coitus

Is difficult to admit. I shed tears of rage. Chasm opens.
In delivering male child

Mothers birth Saturn and Mars of genital savagery,
Murdering progenitors.

I love her like matricide. Death's malignancy enters the room.
I bare fists.

It passes through me to her. She disappears. I weep
For lost possibilities.

*M*OTHER, PROPPED in bed, grows scarlet straining
To move bowels.
A stool would prove kidney function.
Forehead vein protrudes.
"Make a doody?" my sister asks.
Mother assents
But her Depend cradles nothing.
"Afraid not," nurse says.
"Drink," my sister says,
Offering her something.
From under bone overhang, furtively,
We glance at each other,
Muffin, Rick, Daddy, I.
"…Beautiful as ever," my father exclaims.
"Go home, Edward," she retorts.
Catheter tube dry, paper nest eggless.
She relates to smiley face on wall.
Beams at chocolate pudding.
Nephrologist at nurse's station
Informs kidneys have failed.
Dialysis not possible.
Tried everything.
On tubes she has ten,
Without, two.
One of us wants to lie, to say,
"Chin up. You're fine. Home soon."
She has taken her last shit,
Urinated her final jet,
Walked her ultimate step.
No joy awaits.
She decides to pull the plug.
(She persists six days
Filling with toxins, internally itching.
Arms never stretch toward mama.)

*I* **DON'T FEAR** death.
Frankly, I couldn't give a shit.
I'm more anxious about lunch.
We pop such sweat
Petitioning God, that Little Eunuch.
I'm more concerned with hemorrhoids.
My dog feeds ticks,
My refuse rats.
The bloody propane tank.
Martin craves ticket to paradise.
I crave a good crap.
Where bloody hell's the sugar?
The Pope's got a withered pizzle.
Poltroon.
My dick's a throbbing Maserati.
I floor it into women.
Camel, rich man, heaven. Blow it out ass.
I want Glashutte.
Who are these Sikhs and bodhisattvas.
Syphilitic fingered.
Ministers, priests.
I'm off for a pee and corn chips.
I'd rather be Vesuvius dog,
Fire-river sculpted.
I eat trazodone, dream Caribbean,
Perform cunnilingus on razor blade.
Into room protrudes death's frog face.
I smash it with snow globe,
Pack it in verse for verisimilitude.
Life, Buster Brown, is opportunism.
Top club—bloody—and bread pudding.
Once to soften a woman's cunt I sat before her Rinpoche
Who delivered dripping platitudinous crap.

I almost puked.
I spend mutual orgasms like Catholic contrition.
Death's less horrifying than a puppy
Nibbling finger.
I smoke euphoria like heroin.

*D*EATH MUGS me. I moan all day.
Meat on eye.
I double on ground.
It steel-toe kicks me.
Sputum strings.
I'm human pain.
I'm numb, affectless.
Unresponsive.
Glazed abstraction.
I speak vaguely, dispassionately.
Death assaults me behind dumpster.
Knuckle-punches spine.
I grunt and continue grunting.
Antidepressants flatten
But grinding awakens.
I'm bitter, loveless.
I hate the celebrated.
Suddenly Death in back seat materializes,
Pistol whips.
I moan
To market
Which I disgruntled enter.
Fucking Coca Cola.
Fucking lunatics.
I condemn pesticides.
My assailant's a splattered hive.
It swarms, stings.
I down Benadryl.
I drag fat through ketchup.
At night on black streets
My green phosphor monster
Wielding human leg bone
Bashes skull.

Gashing wife's slumber
Into night I shout, "No!"
My impotent spontaneous furious rebuttal.

*M*UFFIN DASHES to foyer.

Quick! She's dying!

We scamper to her room.

One hails a nurse

who appears with stethoscope,

Fixes it over heart.

"Five," she says.

"Mommy, Mommy," yanks out my gut.

I haven't said Mommy in sixty years.

Mommy!

I love you, Mommy.

I'm here, Mommy,

It's okay, Mommy.

Let go, Mommy.

No more suffering.

Mommy, mommy.

I'm four.

I dog her.

I'm in her walk-in.

I'm in her bathroom.

She's curling lashes.

I'm tootling hall.

A vacuum awaits.

Airlessness.

She looks like mashed potatoes.

I stroke hair.

Muffin strokes face.

"Mommy," projectile vomits from her.

We're squabbling.

She's six. Sadistic. Cruel.

Teases me.

Stomps my ingrown toenail.

"Mommy!" I scream.

Exasperated, Mommy appears
Like a Halloween witch.
Slams door.
She'd rather not bother.
Horrible mistake.
Daddy in background doesn't touch her,
knows she'd hate it.
Lets us touch.
Five.
Five beats.
Unfathomable.
Five beats.
I'm four. Mommy twenty-eight.
She takes me to Brucie's.
We bowl indoor pins
While pumped on Johnny Horton.
She, Gloria giggle in kitchen.
Lead cube Death smokes people like Winstons,
Knocks off ashes.
Brucie, Gail, Richard, Robert, John, Todd,
Smile behind my birthday Huffy.
Mommy snaps Polaroid.
I don't know. I don't know a lot.
I know I'm no poet.
I'm a disillusioned jackass who bought his lies.
I'm dirty coal to genius's pure fire.
Now she's a thing
With stopped cold blood.
It's instantly fish.
Its face locked rictus.
They'll have to crack jaw.
Its brain sticks in aspic.
She's nonexistent.

How would Browning or Tennyson put it?

Muffin, Daddy, Darren, I gather round corpse.

"Still beautiful," Daddy blurts.

I agree but don't care.

Her last words, "Of course!" forgave my sins.

She's shoved off the cliff.

"She's dying! Come! Quick!" My sister cries.

We rush.

Nurse mutters five.

My shoe's untied.

No ice fills my spine.

Daddy isn't bawling.

Muffin's forehead's shiny.

Mother's not wire, nor I receiver.

Something cut power.

Fresh bedding. Vacant room. Quiet whirring.

Why vortices? Why funnels?

Only the pull knows the answer.

*T*AKES HER the same time that lovers' two
week Cancun vacation takes: she home
to hospital, they to home to terminal;
she admitted, they checked in; hospital-
routine-she, jet-skis-they; she to hospice,
they to spa; she dead, they home collapsed
on sofa. The dying shallowly cheek-puff,
lovers orgasm-moan, she tolerates soft,
they gorge prawn risotto. Four AM: I whir
downtown past shrouded edifices to that
cube of industry on whose sixth she
languishes. Shoreline Drive, Corpus Christi,
street lights blinking, soft leather buckets
to bedside vigil, throat pounding. Here,
they raised me—Pirates, Troop 218, Ray
High, confirmation—now piloting her
CTS, ghostly palm trees, gray bay glittered
with jack-ups, socket where mighty coliseum
stood. Memories pop, flutter like ashes.
Though progressing I'm not moving, car
in suspended animation, precious silver
Cadillac, hometown rarely visited, dilapidation.
Our hypothetical lovers 69-ing in Oxnard—
lubrication, ejaculation—and I frozen,
blocked, perceiving but not blinking, face
stopped in mid-amazement, fists locked,
arms braced as if squealing toward collision.

## DEATH SUCKS

Death is a shit-kick

Death makes me puke

Death is an emetic

Death bites the big one

Death fucks up everything

Death can eat my dick

Death is red nougat

Death is neonate's hazy blues

Death is tan puppy

Death is LZ Huey dust

Death is sex, *ménage a trois*

Death is chocolate cake batter on lipstick

Is the fold in female genitalia

Is the absence of antecedent

Is Euclidean mathematics

Death is macaw squawk over Playa Bejuco

Death is torrid sand

Death is absence of equal sign

Death is shoo-goo

Death is a pineapple finial maple bed

Death is voiding in a rock concert potty

Death is moral absolutism coupled with gonorrhea

Death is a plate of sizzling enchiladas served to blubbering gastronome

Death is a calamine dipped cotton swab smeared over site of amputation

Death is Virginia Woolf, fearful symmetry, Davy Crockett, Donald's nephews

Death is cheese steak in Boonton with a lethal blonde who does it dog style
        under clattering window unit in August torpor of a late afternoon

Death is dirty lube gnashed between teeth of hydraulic car crusher

Death is a clean technology lab

Death is the arc clasped hands describe between best girlfriends skipping down
        Palisades Avenue en route to the Bijou

Death is spoon-whipping Special K, sugar, half & half into sweet white froth, is dungarees, Track Star shoes, lunch money, heartbroken mother, extreme unction, extraordinary rendition, butch wax flip, and the whole bloody arsenal of black cats, blaster tubes, moon travelers, cherry bombs, sky rockets, and fiery irises

Death is oil smell emitted by the Daisy pump action BB gun in a junkyard outside Robstown, Texas, whipping tiny hearts off blasted branches and engine blocks

Death is a twelve character integer divisible but by self and 1, like the bioluminescent deep sea jelly pulsing past its lure-flash struck by hapless predator in the magical toolbox of the world

Death is routine delivered by trench coat comedian smashed on gin delivering diatribes on the subject of queers, bestiality, monogamy, blow jobs, revenge, AIDS, the pope, masturbation, and sub-Saharan children the instant before their stomachs burst

Death is baby robin redbreast, biologically perfect, lovingly fed, suitably resilient, shifting, neck-stretching while something sweet softens its straw and something irresistible sharpens its blood and something inexorable spills it forth into the brilliant landscape of rustle and song

Death is F-22 raptor in vertical ascent, ass over cone, reverse looping, roaring treetop level upside down, rolling, ripping the hot bed-sheet of sky, vanishing in a tiny white spark, god suction, leaving behind a seductive blue crystalline hunger

Death is the paper, ink, glue of the collected literary classics pulped by massive hammering cylinders into vats of sticky mash employed to mortar concrete blocks into monstrous monuments to vanity and immortality

Death is butt fuck

Is barium enema

Is onomatopoeia

Death is pencil grinder

Is muscular gut

Is double whammy

Death is earthworm's reproductive implantation in glutinous hermaphroditic ooze fusing to clitellum spermatozoa pearls of transparent pupas, spit to spit, gut to gut in a repulsive antediluvian reproductive glue

Death is punch line emitted from hearer, like air squeaking from neck of balloon, an involuntary squeal at ceremony's conclusion complete with liquor and sucked

yellow wedges in a private room decorated with plastic tropical trees and
  blue luminous rope tubes
Death is incessant patriotic productivity: blaster, borer, driller, grinder; thruster,
  crusher, stamper, molder; shearer, cutter, hammerer, lifter pounding,
  slamming, pulsing, showering in red brick mill bisected by train or
  industrial truck hauler tunneling through sooty rimless dreams into the
  hot dawn of day
Death is Revell model airplane kit, pair of tongs, regular boy's haircut, bat-
  tleship Oklahoma, Kaiser's granite castle, turtle carapace, eighteen
  emu eggs, baby's first tooth like oral ice cube, fresh stain, the absence
  concomitantly of nothing and everything, ejaculation of ketchup atop
  moat of potatoes ringing pulled pig, St. Bonobos of Annunciation's mud
  and bone hut, pornographic effigies of adolescent girls nailed to blasted
  trees, Federal Express packages dispatched from trenches to bustling
  kitchens, long transparent snakes of the emaciated and forsaken, sweet
  pickle relish slathered on athletics, the last Mohican splattered across
  field, fist clutching hatchet, cuts of world voluptuously displayed under
  red fluorescence, poets from universities emerging push-headed and pie-
  eyed like a hatchery of idiots
*Camptown ladies sing this song*
*Doo-da doo-da*
*Camptown racetrack's five miles long*
*Oh de, doo-da day*
Death's God's pilot point pen, point un-hooded, chamber loaded, scrawling
  freeway-wide mortification across the world
Death's a young wifely Cordon Bleu gourmet preparing for her warrior garlic
  rubbed chicken, braised Bosque pears to strains of Debussy in her lemon
  curd Lexington, Massachusetts, saltbox kitchen in felicitous yellow
  weather punctuated by songbirds and high sighing pines
Is tire-littered hillside
Is red Ducati 848 straddled by leather-suited goggled screaming blue meanie
  plowing through blaze
Is a young man's meteoric rise to prominence in the public relations game in an

indispensable center for art, finance, and industry, flooded with astonishment, electricity, charisma, zeal, full of virtuosity and affability, connoisseurship and exoticism, generosity and quickness, spinning round narcissism's wheel of mirrors, our hero chock-headed full and beautiful promoted and pampered, recognized, enfolded, catapulted to the penultimate level with two bedrooms, view, partakes of opera and avant-garde cinema in a licked-smooth couture of informal cool, is his purchase, comfort, and security won through passion, tenacity, and self-glorification

Is a perfect day at the Lido

Death is hepcat ginned on jazz vibrating off coffee house pillow on pull and glad curling a dirty copy of Planet News, brain rotating inside skull like sparking magneto switched on high throwing verbiage and nerves into outer realms on a burn-out current of omnipotence and surge

Death is rocking on a paint-peeling porch in Crookneck, West Virginia, on a blowzy cloud-scudded pecan tree afternoon in throat-orange Autumn, meditating on death's slow procession up fragile extremities—fingertips, knuckles, eyelids, lips—finally worming the whole with a thick sweet numbness so drowsy and full it drops in a thud like a heavy rotten pear

Death is *the most beautiful sound I've ever heard/all the beautiful sounds of the world in a single word/I've just met a girl named/I've just kissed a girl named/and suddenly I've found/how wonderful a sound/I'll never stop/playing and praying/ will never be/can be/me*

Death is just as Mary bends to creek for water-drink, God flying into womb like a fighter jet bombing blood, strafing cheeks, embarrassment blushing cheeks like bees, woman of women, queen of queens, carrying that horrifying violence to Galilee for a mass bath of courage and fear, crushing with love blindness, menstruation, leprosy, death like shattered doll pieces flown together into prayer

is the Advance Clean, Optic White, Max Fresh, Peroxide Bubbling, Triple Action, Plaque Control, Gum Protection, Clean Night Mint, Anti-gingivitis, Anti-tartar, Anti-halitosis, Anti-cavity, Clean Cinnamon, Super Invigorating, Pro-Whitening, Health For Me, Luminous, Sensitive, Radioactive, Complete, Stain Defense, Enamel Strengthening, Mentadent, Baking Powder Action, Sodium Fluoride, Wicked Fresh, Botanically Bright, Embrace the Power, All-in-One, Super-Erotic, Natu-

rally Ecstatic, Exquisitely Orgasmic, Immortally Cosmic, Black Light
Irradiating, Milky Way Shattering, God-Interpenetrative, Bubbly Green
Minty-Gel blast

Is the unblemished, without defect, immaculate slaughtered goat

Is blasted apart, disemboweled, truncated; cut down, decapitated, roasted; blown
smithereens, cool-aided, greased; lit up, wasted, X'd; chopped down,
zapped, clotheslined; dirt-napped, peanuted, trashed; iced, broken-
hearted, betrayed; destroyed by lies, devastated by sleaze, lacerated by
duplicity; remorseless, irresistible, addictive; joyous, exquisite, free

Death is turkey, blessing, thanksgiving, pearl onions, family, bean casserole,
laughter, best china, pumpkin mincemeat pecan, flickering plump faces,
glinting crystal, nippy Cleveland satiation, Robert, Paula, Tommy,
Grandpapa, Aunt Sophie, Uncle John, baby Jamie, little Dean, gag-
gling passel, women in kitchen, men on sofa, Buckeyes vs. Wolverines,
Budweiser Toyota Rock of Gibraltar, four air-tight walls, ceiling, floor,
swirling blood-red window, bring on leftovers, jelly belly jollity in man-
ger of love

Is postman, appraiser, Billy Shakespeare

*Hey diddle diddle, cat in fiddle,*

*cow jump over moon*

Is six answers to six questions, hexagram, avalanche of ketchup, six swinging
hooks

Death is I don't know

Who gives a damn

What fuck difference

I'm sick of this, I'm sick of much

Sick of foreknowledge

Prescience

Fear

Neurosis

Majordomos

Footmen

Penitence

Atonement

Mortification

Contrition

Self-contamination

Humility

Interdiction

Compunction

Frugality

Deprivation

Grackle cackle

Gustatory restraint

Mirror embarrassment

Hell dreams

Reckless fantasies

Entombing facades

Merciless civilities

Lentil soup

Egotistical edifices

This year's prize winners

Fat blockers

Marathon runners

Spinning machines

Damnation by blasphemy

Salvation by conformity

Squeaky chairs

Cemeteries

Petrification

Dehydration

Fossilization by imitation

Farcical Seders

Unity Church

Opportunists of entropy

Perfection and its attendant clamp-jaw

Everyone's brilliance

Anxiety, palpitations, compulsions, medications

Fish's final spasm in fiberglass hull

Mother passing, Daddy crossing nine months hence

Talent, talent, the grinding mill-wheel of talent and decay on the other side of
        power in a chair before Martian technology

Death is comedian's failure in blank faces

Comedian setting sail for lost integrity

Comedian on windless clipper delivering punch lines to the sea

And the gonads to continue.

*D*EATH NAILS up pictures like a new tenant.

Death serves red skins with chives.

Death sucks ink out ballpoint tube.

Death likes puppets and zoo conveyances.

Death purchases Bridgestone run-flat tires.

Death solves the Sneaky Pete hand-puzzle.

Death sticks walnut shell on nose, kisses with wax lips.

Death smokes garter snakes with BB gun.

Death mainlines semen like junkie.

Death's a fool for hockey, raw oysters.

Death loves bald eagles and patriotic gewgaws.

Death collects presidential bobbleheads.

Death bursts two quivering Buddhas on toast.

Military is a euphemism for red licorice.

Two-sticker Hi-Flier American Beauty kite.

Cat fur in pinto beans.

Fairfield County Courthouse's gleaming balustrades.

Lingeringly, Death pees in the Royal Plaza Suite.

"Mosaic tiles, Sherle Wagner faucets."

Death crawls under legs, fellates a goat.

Ten Astroglide-slick Pininfarina cylinders.

Death is grinding drill head hitting gusher.

Dalrymple's Darling Dancing Demons.

Death dashes the 100 backward into a rushing-forward future.

With grinning head wedged between ankles Death rocks on tummy.

Voraciously, Death licks solicitation envelopes. Chin dribbles glue.

Death rips flesh off skeleton in g-force experiment.

I fortify pancakes with woodpecker and gunpowder.

Brush fire ignites edges of Death's mauve tutu.

Plangent, plaintive, plundering, pabulum.

Death eats Harry Truman like a pig knuckle.

I pencil sharpen death's head in a flatulent platypus.

Death leaves Jupiter fingerprints on glass bludgeon.

Lemon curd.

Spit and blood mutilate Death's Oberammergau flesh.

Death scrawls its autobiography on toilet water.

I perform anal sex between Death's buttocks.

I suck its male tit. Sludge gushes.

Its dick shoots sour cream through fingers.

Death cleans prawn intestine with tongue.

Under the Christ-tree Death rat skitters, morphed into a pretty package for Polly.

I'm primed for Tommy Merton & The Shondells.

Puddle at nib-tip after Esterbrook's suddenly terrified bladder.

What think you, drunken mussels or haberdashery clams?

Death swallows steel cable, waits three days, flosses intestines.

Death's a three-duck-head blaring air raid siren.

Shattering fragile crystal of kicked testicles.

Butch Hair Wax flip gets Hush Puppy love at Bill's Shoe Box.

Whoops.

In one blow innocence strings out Death's nose leaving it airless, addicted, croaking,
    alone. Death drags off leaving a slime trail.

Death's thrusting solid fuel binky corkscrews Death down hell like a Texas Twister.

Frog snaps Death's flipping tiddlywink before it squops little Timmy.

Molly, good golly! Joe Bazooka, Penny King, baking powder submarine.

Death files thumb nail on the Hoover Dam, scrubs teeth with mountain peaks, and in
    between apoplectic crusades bathes in the Mariana Trench.

Squeeze-honks miniature trike horn while pedaling under rumps, red plastic wig.

Look says Death, wiggles ears.

Now you're riveted, watch, it says, and pulses nostrils.

Betcha can't do this, it taunts, turns round and back: all eye whites.

For my grand finale, it announces, and

Locks arm wrenched off socket behind neck, stiff, palm forward.

Every trick I try I reeks with incompetence.

*I* LEAVE HER deathbed vigil to run.
For a geezer I cover good ground.
The hospital recedes,
Illuminated cube.
I run toward dusk.
My knees ache; I'm graceless.
I pass Cole Park, littered dump.
I cross Naples, Southern, Louisiana
With its dilapidated antebellum mansions.
I ache, persist.
I need air, relief from decomposing flesh.
I need distance, natural hue.
I need to experience functioning lungs.
I piss behind a hummock. I live in urinative crisis.
I left my sister flossing mother's teeth.
She performs intimate offices
I find repugnant.
Birds abound, crows, grackles, gulls squawk in heavy weather.
I U-turn at First Baptist Church with its
Neo-Spanish tower.
How much longer can she last?
Renal failure.
She still eats, sips.
I'm not dead but damnably sore.
Senescent.
Back across Naples, Southern, Louisiana
In reverse order
Away from sun.
I don't know how to feel.
I'll inherit money.
I can remodel.
I'll have no mother.
The warped dependency will fade. I already miss it.

I enter the refrigerated Christmas lobby.

Push number 6.

Ironically, she delivered me in this facility.

I'm now that infant.

Quietly, I push the door.

My sister sits against wall.

Mother dozes.

Oxygen whirs.

Rick shuttled Daddy home.

"Dinner?," I whisper.

*"Donde esta?"* she inquires?

"The Acapulco. Cheese enchiladas!"

*M*Y BROTHER-IN-LAW commands, "Lie, convey
hope, remind her the restorative power
of optimism." "They said," I respond, "she'll
be dead in a week, this truth is hers, not
ours to withhold." "Untrue," he says, "let
her die with dignity, untroubled by dread."
"Who are you," I demand, "to refuse a
human final introspection?" Inside I'm
livid, take the conflict outside. "She'll have
the truth, I'll speak it." "Mother," I say,
"your kidneys have failed, the doctor said
there's nothing she can do. This will be
fatal." The thorn gashes its own petal.

*D*OCTOR ASKS if we want to keep her tubes in. We
ask her. She does not. She wants unplugging,
conveyance to hospice, death. She's sick of it.
Mitral regurgitation, valve clicking, prostration,
doctors doctors doctors. She's ready. Yes,
unplug. Remove me. She's still eating but
eliminating nothing. Collecting inside. Renal
failure. Try, we say. She strains beet red. I
think I did, she beams, but she hasn't. Empty
diaper. Okay, then. Itching internally, she
cracks a joke, I'm itch bitch! All her life she
enjoyed friends. Bridge, canasta. Unceasing
tingling. Sylvia. Madeline. Miriam. Viv. She's
resolute. Bumped in on gurney feet first. Where
we going? Better place. Ok. Sturdy Stryker.
Shiny night streets, steel-walled ambulance
enclosing trauma. Take care of Daddy—to
me, to Rick. Promise you'll take care of Edward.
First words at hospice. Promise, we say. She
eats little, then nothing. We capture water
in soda straw, with finger release between
lips. Tender the nurses, kindhearted, sweet.

*H*E DARE NOT touch her. He knows she loathes him. Instead fidgets beside bed. Her disgust has distorted behavior: the less affection, the more he yammers. He blathers to her malignant displeasure. She winces, suggests he take a nap. "Rick, take him home." Rick's no idiot. Rick knows he loves her. Will she recover or is this death? We think the latter. *It's been a long time coming.* "Mother it would mean everything if you'd let him take your hand." She does later, but painfully. Revulsion overwhelms her. Banished but not gone he stands peripherally, chattering. A leather driver's cap smashes his head. She hasn't touched him in decades. Ejecting us all to expunge just him she requests solitude. Rick takes him home. She worsens, stops eating, is pronounced terminal, is transferred to hospice, languishes, expires. She never again repels him. In nine months he goes from chatter to prattle to gibber to drool, then morphine-stunned dies on a strange bed, gasping.

*D*EATH IS rat nibbling in kitchen. Skitters
Across floor down toilet to river, city's
Black river, whip-tail locomotion through
Pollution to sewer, it shits and shits.

Death is song wedged in head, lacerating
Brain like a razor ball, nail lacquer glossy,
Menstrual blood rich, chronic as rickets,
Angrily, it slices eyeballs in its exit.

Death is mutilated feet of homeless junkie,
Delicate flesh peeled, stripped badge of
Dereliction. Five filthy blood bulbs swollen
Beneath sticks. The eye in each weeps.

Death is wedding resembling bucket of
Cow placenta quivering like black Jell-O
While calf suckles, creek water trickles—
A floral breeze prefigures the coronation.

Death is barber's cold electric razor driven
Up back of childhood neck exposing white
Raw flesh, clip-littered bib, audacious bulging
Head of subjection, outrage, fear, insurrection.

Death is smoke alarm's sadistic red button
Floating behind brain-curtain, bursting
Tranquility, threatening through night's
Velvet piercing blasts of low battery life.

Death is perfect apple with adorable stem,
Sitting on sepal like an upside-down king,
Asymmetrical, plentiful, splitting it cleanly

In one vengeful whack, Eve's disobedience.

Is cube in gin dissolving round pit. Is beak
Plunged in blood. Is watch ticking round
Nostalgia of wrist. Is pilot's nosebleed. Is
Love's exegesis disemboweled, steaming.

*M*Y FISTS FLY up reflexively before my face beside her bed, like grotesque architecture—pig iron claws—locked, flexed, raking something: threat without enemy, rage without source, raking air, she is slipping, unresponsive, skull emerging, Munch's reverberation, I sinking nails into cold imaginary clay, into death's flesh. She gasps. She fish-puffs cheeks. Eyeballs crust over. Psycho violin screeches. I lacerate something. Claws stuck up like incinerated soldier's. I cannot be mere grieving human, but squeezed choler, hands in spasm, she is neither eating nor shitting. We feed her soda straw captured water. My sister squabs her lips. Nurses flitter in, out, some with Benadryl. Can she hear? "We're here," we say. "We love you." Resistance jags down my arms rigidifying hands, fingers locked, sections raw, inside I seep like punctured gas, bare fists. I am chastised. I am diminished. I am repentant. I am insect, exoskeleton, walking stick. Her lips bristly stitches. Black crusts her temples. Her body a self-constructing casket. She was tough avaricious vulture. Death is tougher. My hands fly up before my face, beside her bed, defying nothing. Ghosts. An unresponsive mother, an impotent son, a burnt twisted pig iron sculpture of spit and acid in a hospice room.

"**F**ORGIVE ALL the pain I caused," at her bedside,

I beg.

"I was awful.

I apologize."

She is dying.

It is 2:00 AM.

She lies semi-conscious in hospice gown,

Laboring, voiceless,

Two weeks into renal failure,

Misshapen,

Internal torture,

Eighty-eight,

Blood pooling,

That ominous shallow fish-puffing.

I know she hears.

Curtains diffuse street lamp.

Horror smell.

The broken promise

Of oxygen tube

Slipped off ear.

My sins were legion:

Lousy student,

Drunkard,

Drag racer,

Three abortions,

Four marriages,

Emotional misfit,

Financial cripple,

Constantly uprooting,

Embarrassment

Against her friends'

Exemplary scholars,

Evincing, undoubtedly,

Private agony.
As I scrunch into pallet,
Untwist pajamas after
Erasing myself across the room,
"Of course!" she shatters.

*I* CYCLE IN and out her room.

I employ guest computer.

I watch nephew work iPad brain twisters.

I phone wife.

I think today's the day, I say.

I think it's time.

It's horrific.

I want to be home.

I'm finished with poetry.

I want to appreciate life.

I'm withdrawing my grotesque book of anger.

I'm through with agitation. Screw torture.

Let's take a trip. Expand.

Shanghai.

We have but moments.

I plan to believe in God.

I cycle back to her room,

Silent scream, like pawnbroker.

She lays quiescent.

A swamp her neck.

Lumpy dumpling face.

She had sorority lips.

She had red misandrist nails.

I sit beside morphine paste-pot.

I cycle out, land beside my sister.

Her two adult children don't empathize.

She's antiquarian, they're charging.

I like them.

One cares marginally.

My sister's husband appears.

This is it, I say.

Let's go in.

Silently we enter, afraid to wake baby.

Hushed tones.

Nestling.

Hair fuzz.

She's been through hell.

I hope she goes.

So do I.

Daddy's nonplussed.

"Still beautiful gal, day we met.

Storybook marriage.

Won't know how to live without."

He doesn't touch her.

She hasn't permitted it for decades. He's conditioned. She's smoking ice.

Storybook.

A driver's cap smashes his head.

Rick sprawls in chair.

My sister despises Rick. Thief, she claims.

Maybe. Who cares.

She refuses his bonus.

Anyway, he's promised to Daddy.

My sister dashes from Mother's room.

She dying! Quick!

We rush.

Nurse with stethoscope says 5.

We stroke her face.

Mommy.

Mommy.

Then zero.

She passes. Mouth agape.

Blur:

Morticians.

Coffin.

Meeting.

Papers.

Burial.

Guests.

Reception.

Bank check.

Obituary.

Newspaper.

Death is enterprise.

Reminiscences.

Finally, just Daddy, Muffin, Larry, me. We go to bed. Daddy weeps all night.
     Weeps for nine months, dies.

Rick loves him more than we.

My sister's rigid and practices unblemished morality.

Rick, she says, stole linen.

I spoon shredded wheat. Read box. No sugar.

Rick arrives at 5:45 AM, chauffeurs me to terminal.

I love you, I say. His heart's big.

Crappy stores fly by.

I procure ticket, check bag, sip coffee.

Clean brilliant cheerful port.

Jet detaches from earth like lover off lips.

Wheels bump in.

It shudders, roars.

A thin fear like alcohol fume

fills my brain.

I'm five years old. I've forgotten moving day.

I dash home to mommy from kindergarten school.

The door is locked.

Nobody stirs.

I sit on the stoop

Of a gutted house

Abandoned, bawling.

*I* GUIDE DADDY'S left arm through sleeve,
Pull shirt round bony back,
Slide in right arm.
Bare feet flat on floor he sits
On bed, chastised child.
I button from bottom leaving collar ajar.
I bend, bunch left trouser leg
And thread foot through.
Bunch and repeat with right.
"Stand," I say.
"Look what's happened to me."
"Not so bad," I say. "Stand."
Arthritically he stands.
I wedge shirttail into pants
And fasten round belly alligator belt.
Trousers slide off.
"Uh oh," I laugh.
I unbuckle belt, re-hitch pants, secure on tighter notch.
"Sit," I command.
"Sit?"
"Yeah, sit."
I unroll sock up left foot.
Repeat with right.
Shiny nylon.
"Okay," I say. "Good."
Now, let's button the collar."
The starched button hole grudgingly submits.
Tie flows over hand like water.
Conservative blue diamond.
I bump up collar, wrap round tie, pop down collar, even ends,
Tie the four-in-hand he once taught me,
Botch it, try again.
Over right foot black Florsheim shoe,

54

Mate over left.

Tighten waxed laces.

"Okay, stand."

He stands.

His pants shimmy to slip. I hoist them over egg to nipples.

(Rick supports him, he says, with a fistful of belt.)

I cuff link sleeves,

Slip on jacket.

"God almighty," he ejaculates, consternated.

"Jesus Christ."

My sister entering exclaims, "How nice, Daddy."

I smooth him down

Anxious about pants.

"Ready?"

The house a defunct movie set.

"Where's Sophie Mae?"

"Meeting us there."

"Is Larry here?"

"Kitchen, riding with us."

"Where's Roslyne. She coming?"

"She died, Daddy. We're going to her funeral."

(Long pause, head in hand).

"God, almighty. Horrible situation. I'll survive. I'll be okay."

The house cannot feel.

It exhales heated air.

A window blunts the winter rose.

A brass clock scissors chips.

Brain noise fills the air.

Four people back down the drive.

Miramar to Center to Ocean to Seaside Memorial.

In the car Larry snaps Daddy's buckle.

Zips his fly.

Patted and adjusted, he's ready now to face the mourners.

*I* **AM THIRD** to throw in dirt. It strikes the
coffin with a hollow blow to remain, I
assume, forever there. Three nights later
straddling neck I fuck my wife's mouth
more for solace than ecstasy. I come
on the bones between her breasts.

*H*OW D'YA say goodbye to solid marble egg

How d'ya say goodbye to green ceramic vase

How d'ya say goodbye to garlic press

How d'ya say goodbye to presidential race

How d'ya say goodbye to cat-hair coated vest

How d'ya say goodbye to mauve canvas sneakers

How d'ya say goodbye to flat refrigerator handle

How d'ya say goodbye to cracked bomber jacket

How d'ya say goodbye to Queequeg, Crusoe, Huck

How d'ya say goodbye to heirloom photograph

How d'ya say goodbye to guilt, shame, rage

How d'ya say goodbye to cheeky teenage spunk

How d'ya say goodbye to defiance, rebellion, contempt

How d'ya say goodbye to lightly salted butter

How d'ya say goodbye to interplay of fact and fiction

How d'ya say goodbye to whiff of distant memory

How d'ya say goodbye to self-aggrandizing myth

How d'ya say goodbye to red utility knife

How d'ya say goodbye to swaggering big-hair surfer

How d'ya say goodbye to nostalgia of desperate kisses

How d'ya say goodbye to mother's lipstick tube

How d'ya say goodbye to Pillsbury pastry flour

How d'ya say goodbye to measles, mumps, flu

How d'ya say goodbye to glimpses round corner

How d'ya say goodbye to midnight chocolate cow

How d'ya say goodbye to bristling enemy hatred

How d'ya say goodbye to vivid unfinished vision

How d'ya say goodbye to stomach's hungry gullet

How d'ya say goodbye to ruthlessness, cruelty, greed

How d'ya say goodbye to the opportunity to kill mother

How d'ya say goodbye to after dinner toothpick

How d'ya say goodbye to sumptuous internal ugliness

How d'ya say goodbye to satirizing the Pope

How d'ya say goodbye to megalomania, necrophilia, fantasy of mass extermination

How d'ya say goodbye to inner totalitarianism

How d'ya say goodbye to popped innocent teenage cherry and the innumerable subse-
   quent boozy gropings, conquests, pregnancies, promises

How d'ya say goodbye to velocity-exhilaration

How d'ya say goodbye to needles without veins, utopian tapioca

How d'ya say goodbye to cucumber sass at gathering tragedy: friend's knotted blood
   clot, son's immortality by dope

How d'ya say goodbye to sublime fingers

How d'ya say goodbye to flaming tire stripes

How d'ya say goodbye to pointillist dyslexia

How d'ya say goodbye to dirty splayed deck of aptitude and ability

How d'ya say goodbye to blue donkeys, pink manatees

How d'ya say goodbye to heroic aspiration which plumps like industrial turkey, isolates
   like nuclear waste, scars like jagged glass, impoverishes like bitterness, stereotypes
   like supremacist, and prepares with pop and flash for the human sacrifice

How d'ya say goodbye to messianic oath

How d'ya say goodbye to Buck Rogers, Flash Gordon, Sky King, Lone Ranger

How d'ya say goodbye to imaginary terrapins

How d'ya say goodbye to recognition tenuously dangling

How d'ya say goodbye to Daisy BB gun, Mitchell spinning reel, Puma hunting knife,
   mutual Mentholatum masturbation, plastic basket of fries

How d'ya say goodbye to Nickles banana flip

How d'ya say goodbye to cherry Huffy, playing card spoke-clatter

How d'ya say goodbye to magnificent lust, excruciating ventriloquism

How d'ya say goodbye to sputtering resuscitation, presidential assassination

How d'ya say goodbye to poured caramel of mangled soldiers, charred enemies, pulped
   children, fire-thrown villages, Elvis Pelvis, breeze-twisting martyrs, fire-hosed pro-
   testers, dashed homosexuals, broken nations paved with bones crushed into earth
   atop which we stride accomplished, powerful, invincible

How d'ya say goodbye to majesty's amber sway undergirded by empty sockets

Don't believe it

Can't be real

Inconceivable

Beyond comprehension

How could it

Inexcusable

Fuck this shit

By whose design

How d'ya say goodbye to plaster, laughter echo, ghost, fog, pottery shard, worn
bed sheet, staircase groove, dog hair, slurp, ratty doll, chewed pencil,
flickering wing, bronchial tube, disappointment, elation, birthday balloon,
garbage, scissors, nightmare, world atlas, underarm fat, tongue bud, under-
foot crunch

I'm apoplectic

Disbelieving

Stunned

Infuriated

Primed for action

Running toward, away

Broken

Whole

Renegade

Without succor, explanation, bandage, blame.

*M*OTHER'S LIFE flashes.

No future, only past.

Pamper. Adore. Kiss. Kiss. Worship. Only child. Gentleness. Affection. Sweet
baby.

Depression-era Papa hawking papers. Street. Home late. Asleep in shoes.

Up morning.

Mama knees scrubbing floor.

Grandma 4:00 AM Russian black bread.

Cypress Avenue awake in dark. Madness of livelihood. Sixth grade education.

She bouncing, bounced. Dumpling. Queen.

Papa reciting Kipling, shaving whip cream face. Girl at knee.

Let me see. *If you can keep your head when all about you/If you can walk with
crowds and keep your virtue/…yours is the earth and everything that's/…
and which is more, you'll be a Man, my son!* Woman works.

School books swinging beside pinafore.

Bad valve. Bad heart. Tired in young muscle. In urgency.

Rest. Rest. Rest. Naps. Vanilla pudding. Milk.

Funny, they taught. Sense of humor. But money wins. Big.

But laughter, yes, with money. Papa's parsimony, dime a week in college jar, and
shrewdness, good humor, never worried or imparted same, adored Mama,
adored.

Jolly, and she unimpeachable.

High school Lariat Girl but couldn't sustain rigor.

Fright. Campus. Boys. No. No way. Unhappy. Homework. Home. Home. Home.
Daddy! Kipling. Markham, *Bowed by the weight of centuries he leans/
Emptiness of ages in face/…on his back the burden of the world.* Woman
works. Suffering offspring.

But one, flame, devil, Romeo, gum smacking, smarty pants, sweeper of lily,
(rose more apropos), Kiss, kiss, kiss, chocolates. Daddy, bone in pant,
virgin, untouchable, no way. Doorstep kiss. War.

Man-less campus. Austin, enlistees pouring into streets. Heroes. Saliva. Fear.
Sass. Boy guts. Boy ears. Boy butts. Marching out. Austin. Man-less cam-
pus. Ticket. Ticket. Bus. Devil in blue, Philadelphia, and off I am, unfin-

ished, marriage. Papa.

What's this? (penis). In this? (vagina). Atop who? (me). Never! (Intercourse). Papa. Daddy. Poem. Hoe. If. One and twenty. Anything. Not this. Bloody torturous brutal blunt.

Baby one, baby two. Monsters. Tyrants. Devourers. Nannies perpetual.

Albums. Birthdays. Bicycles. Dolls. Water hose plastic pool. Prince Valiant sword. Rhinestone.

Breakdown. Daddy! Daddy! Daddy! Oh! Daddy! Daddy! Daddy! Oh! Daddy! Daddy! Daddy! Quick!

Depression. Bawling. Bed. Wants to die. Failure. Worthless. Starvation. Homelessness. Daddy help him. Me. Hospital. Convulsive shock. The children. Remove. Away. Bertha's. The business? Prow sinking. Want out! What do I? Am I? Is one? Mistake.

(And the great thick allcolor paint smear of words): Egypt, Costa Rica, Mexico, France, friends, youth, alcohol, football, Miramar, crisis-crisis-crisis-accusation-claw-hate-acid-buildup-failure-ruin-regret-eggs-potatoes-maids-hot rain-magnolias-worms-torpid-canasta-repulsion-revulsion-repugnance-banishment-ice cream soda-wax paper beach sandwiches-sacrifice-dead crabs-shrimp heads-cousins-mama-laughter-insomnia-pills-pills-pills-pills-money-money-schemes-betrayal.

Betrayal, embezzling my dead daddy's laborious triumph over Great Depression. My noble, sainted, generous, compassionate, religious father with your sleazy duplicitous hypocritical underworld brain! Desecrated him, sweat of brow. May he rise from grave and murder you! The nerve! You've trampled it. Wish you were dead.

Antipathy. Animosity. Acrimony. Depthless plunge of human rage. Through, past flesh sheath into infinite fiery miasma. Alienation. Disgust. Expulsion from heat. Wetness. Me. Mr. Rot. Mr. Bastard. Mr. Dead.

Twenty years. Twenty horrible.

Singe.

Shrivel.

Petrification.

Fossil.

Friends.

Atrophy.

Heart plaque.

Witticism.

Fantasy.

Hooked.

Disgrace.

Forbidden.

Vowed.

Helpless.

Courage.

Repression.

Image.

And now this. Renal, heart, excretion seizure. Life leaping me like joyous maggots. Fear. Horror. Helpless. Relief. Children. Don't let him here. Cold. Numb. Blink-less. Hazy. Who's? Where? What? Am I? Is this? Is it? Is? Am? When? Blind? Sensation? Something? Look! See! Great. Black. Bear. Gamboling. Away.

(I love you, I say, I'm here. Goodbye Mommy. Goodbye Mommy. Mommy Goodbye.)

# PART II

*I* AM CALLED to daddy's hospital room, he slumps in chair, head
on chest a rotten melon oozing gibberish, mouth a knife-slash,
Muffin and I study each other, nurse rustles in, out, pain chart
with lemony tears, squeaky shoes, heroics a smashed geranium,
left pit lymphomatous, skin graft head-crater, aspic eyes, this
college prankster, fraternity gimcrack, civic stand-out, black-
faced minstrel, member in perfect attendance, temple president,
trout-slimed angler muttering misshapen syllables, recent
companion to chamber pot, falling down pants, disorientation,
shitted towel, manikin whom caregiver animated, who knows
what movie Daddy's brain throws—doubtless the same conflict,
crisis, heroics, recognition always—mundanity in death's
antechamber—he recoils in pain at minor adjustments, ooh!
ooh! he yelps, we default to inanities: "love you," "wonderful
father", "cherish," "going to see mom," "let go when ready,"
and we regress to abandoned children battling pitiless monster,
how diminished this once terrifying Hercules: scabby legs,
stained nails, wrapped in death's sulfuric shroud, malodorous, cutlass
with tattered sail drifting to harbor through ghostly
fog, captain's bones lashed to wheel—so melodramatic!—merely
the flawed husband, father, working stiff limited by genetics,
competition, creativity at ninety-two in a suburban facility
crammed with counterparts, fuck it, who gives a damn, wiping
snivel on hand in hall like a punished school boy, finally first
morphine tab in a series pulling out stuff like cotton wad,
eyes shocked open, plaster mask, hour upon awful hour, squealing
shoes, through first night and day following, next night and
again day, wet rag application, offspring vigil, blinds blunting
light, oxygen whirring, practical activity of harried staff,
bracketed, insignificant like Icarus's distant splash, sudden
activity blur: morticians wrapping it like Cuban tobacco,
heave-hoing onto cart, strapping it down, sympathetically but
without discretion rolling it past the wracked and abstracted.

I 'M AT REMOTE parking.

I'm on a shuttle.

I'm at the airport.

I'm on a plane.

I arrive in Corpus.

Rick meets me.

We drive to hospital.

Daddy dozes in a room.

He looks like shit.

I greet my sister.

"How is he?"

"He'll survive."

My sister hates him.

I hate him.

Rick tolerates him.

Rick honors the promise he made mother before she died to see him

Through.

Rick's a good man.

My sister shaves daddy.

She brushes his teeth.

She flosses him.

She checks his diaper.

Rick goes home.

We go to dinner.

Enchiladas.

We return, kiss daddy good night.

"Bright and early."

We drive home.

I sleep in childhood bed.

I spoon cold cereal.

We return.

Nothing's changed.

Washed, he mumbles in a chair.

We face him, bereft.

What's he saying?

We study each other.

Days pass.

He dies.

We bury him.

Rick drives me to the airport.

I'm on a plane.

I arrive.

I'm at remote parking.

I'm in traffic snarl.

I kill the engine.

An hour passes.

Zeppelin, Brubeck, Rachmaninoff.

Finally.

It's early evening.

I open the door

Like a salesman home

With sample case.

My wife embraces me.

The house is tidy.

We lay down.

Talk.

I sniffle.

I marvel at how it went from worship to repression to odium.

My heart a cold mop.

The boy inside me blinks ancient lids.

The eyes inside daddy stopped blinking.

I awake.

Same furniture, same arrangement.

Same oddments.

I'm getting fat.

I breakfast on oatmeal, 2 percent.

Mother died 9 months ago.

They were married 68 years.

She despised him.

He knew it.

He died with strong vitals

Of a broken heart.

The wrecked marriage

Leaves a legacy,

I cry a week before I stop.

Life isn't perfect.

I never fought in war.

Some would say how unfortunate.

No sense in self-sacrifice,

Nationalism.

I'm capable of extreme detachment.

My father typed in WW2.

Philadelphia.

I roam the house.

I graze for snacks.

I read a book: **A Bright Shining Lie.**

My wife and I make love.

Sixty-three is a libidinous age.

Youth believes frost crinkles old brows, that life's winter brings sexual

Cessation.

What crap!

It *is* snowing

But I'm rutty as hell.

Daddy is irrelevant.

Mother is immaterial.

Death is extraneous.

Self is universe.

I am empathic and yet

Survivors of tragedy

Insult the dead.

Mother lies beside Daddy in perpetuity.

When slicing his grave

Her liner peeked through into his.

I am agnostic.

I have no proof.

I love art house film.

Last night I survived a nuclear blast

By crouching behind a concrete pillar.

The force blew me backward

Onto a friend

I could move my legs.

Two coddled eggs wobble in cup

Like joyful Buddhas

I burst with spoon.

The yolk is warm

And peppery to tongue.

I respect the dead

By striding atop them.

*D*EATH STRADDLING red Ducati slingshots through successive aces.
Death recedes to a dot, roars back in a rocket hail decimating village.
Death guzzles cow blood through industrial funnel.
Death births hermaphroditic worm which delivers milky wrigglers.
Death bolos a power wire with laced-together sneakers.
As acclaimed in Soldier of Fortune Magazine, Death chops off enemy's
    knuckles.
Death cascades inside sprayed herbicide.
Death consoles sobbing survivor.
Death squirts goo, performs proctology.
Death's Dick Van Dyke's mercurial hassock.
Death wipes ass, stuffs soiled paper in Kleenex box.
Death arranges Lily of Valley, constructs the wedding cake.
Dominant male ape hauls boxes for subdominant female mate.
Homunculus Death squashes insect under fingertip.
Death napalms Gomorrah by blowing its nose from a jet.
Sodom's mayors notice and plunge into whores' gushing flesh.
Death adores cream cheese caper triangles, crust removed.
Death's Octopus smashes together screaming children.
Baxter seizes toxic chop tossed over Death's privacy fence.
Out pubic swamp vaults giant sequoia Death masturbates like a Texas
    gusher.
Death's wife pounds it down it like Jell-O.
Death reciprocates by downing gallon of orange GoLYTELY.
Death plays solitaire with deck of gas chamber victims.
Death corn holes crack addict, feasts on nipples.
Death whistles Yankee Doodle while broiling itself in an industrial oven.
Death plucks mudslide-suffocated children like Peter Piper picking pep-
    pers.
From fourth stomach Death regurgitates food ball of its mother.
Jury Death hears accused Death questioned by prosecutor Death, repairs to
    Death's antechamber, emerges, finds Death guilty, whereupon Judge
    Death condemns Death to death by lethal injection.

Madman Death laughs out loud, eats prison rats.

Death's psychotherapist offers Death floral blubber box.

Death dams voltage, throws switch.

God plunges trowel in Death, mortars edifice.

Burnt to un-recognition Death sodomizes farmer's cow, sow, baby, wife,
    then douses sin with gasoline.

Death's spin cycle torques skin off rocks.

Between Death and tomorrow prance plaster horses.

Between yesterday and Death blooms cranium crocus.

Through Johnny's eye flies slingshot rock which penetrates brain, sprouts
    Death vine.

The bloody baby slides into palms of Doctor Death.

Around its naked bottom wrap Death's latex fingers.

Alpha Bravo Charlie incinerates sky. Terrified Death cowers in comrade's
    guts.

Cadmium red kisses cobalt blue through a silicone net.

Nestling robin opens gullet to wormy Death.

Whose flukes flat-slap ocean crest?

God's son Death wiggles tongue through knot hole.

God's son Death slurps slime off flopping fish.

God's son pops bucket of fried roaches.

Death retracts glacier back into gullet. Locks lips.

Horsefly Death…

——Oh fuck this shit. Screw it. Can't do this anymore. Who needs it? I'm
    no poet. I'm charlatan, poseur, crackpot, fake. Walking lie. Piss on it.
    I need bath bomb, hedonism, the Presidential suite. Poetry is Death.
    Forty death-years. Forty years wall-bashing. Forty years impene-
    trable establishment, intolerable hell people—dandies, interlopers,
    prima-donnas, prigs. Forty years shoving hot poker up ass. For what?
    Separation? Adulation? Veneration? Fame? This is a suicide note,
    monoxide hose, Nembutal overdose. I'm in brain seizure. Sun's flam-
    ing out. It's snowing on The David. Ice age Poetry freezing joy solid?

Death's not poison, attrition, tumor, collision, but Poetry itself. The lure.
The promise. The spasm. The smashing. I'm finished——

Poetry can-cans under puppeteer Death's whimsical fingers.

*I*'M A DING *dong daddy from Dumas you oughta see me do ma stuff!* He booms, his Popeye chant. Might as well bulge a bicep. Referring, I think, to titanic achievement, expectation—self-love afire. It's late 50s. We watch Davy Crockett, Freddie Freeloader, retire, and in the morning: *I'm ding dong daddy Dumas...."* He bursts two yolks with toast. I don't question. He's the kind of bloke who pushes noses in piss, who, fists bared, rushes people. Destruction by minutia. Stuffed with ego. But he is failing, married to Frigidaire. Doing stuff a joke. Now he's dying, dribbling nonsense from lolling tongue, dementia-eaten, and Muffin and I sit beside in visible discomfort. Periodically she strokes his face. We both despise him but emote. Vultures eat. He never again opens eyes, within a week dies. Demise of Popeye, a lifeless papery concave goat, ear tufts, jaw locked round gaping hole. Lip-less. All my life that song floated to brain like an eight-ball fortune. Still does. *Daddy, Dumas, do ma stuff, ding dong* at oddest hours, guzzling Coke, having sex. I gaze upon corpse. No forearm tank, no bicep howitzer. They wheel him out, I bid adieu. Anticlimactic. It's

just Rabbi, Muffin, me, and a few
disconnected stalwarts. He was
vice-president of the Sammies.

*D*EATH'S PRESENCE being strongest in love, lovers
interpenetrate manically, everyplace on their
itinerary, incessantly hammering, spike in pliant
wood, with or without contraceptive, savagely,
tum-to-tum. Death pops out navel like hissing
gas, steams them up. Afterward the abyss, two
sapiens undesirably unstuck. Death's amused
lips. They barricade—phalanx of money, muscle,
offspring, gifts jammed and mortared six feet
thick, Death passes though like vented air into
sanctum of heroism & thrust where they go
at it uncontrollably, death sits on chest like
bowling ball, love being death's antithesis the
two blow each other white hot, death smothers
kisses with Novocain, love entombs death
with solder lead, love's battalions in a frenzied
scrum rally round rose, valentine, Whitman
Sampler; death injects strychnine into love.

MUFFIN CONVICTS daddy of betrayal.
He embezzled her inheritance.
Mother signed papers he thrust before her,
His secretary forged her name to checks.
He gave money to slime balls
Who promised favors.
He showered money to look big,
One million over ten years
Of megalomania.
He liquidated annuities.
When discovered he threatened to blow off his head.
Mother expunged him.
From that moment all despised him.
Guilt like a grater
Slivered his bones.
Electroconvulsive therapy,
Dalmane, Haldol, Miltown, Librium.
His wife ate Valium.
She dead, he now lies in hospice bed
Demented beyond imagining
Wasted, heaving.
Muffin and I reassure him,
"Great daddy, wonderful man, we're here, love you."
Muffin trades tears for fuck you finger.
I dab eyes.
Who knows what epithets inhabit Dad:
Hero? Prophet? Genius? God?
Muffin straightens sheet, check's diaper, buzzes nurse.
I study his pate's cratered skin graft.
One of us thinks fucker,
The other tragedy.
I smear him with paint,
Yellow rage.

Black hate.
Green grief.
Within minutes
Death's spider bundles him.

I saw no soul escape his breast
But mother exited his back
Like a thousand daggers.

*S*PACE AGE plastic glinting helmet of
wide receiver, rubber cleated
human Testarossa runs cross-pattern,
turns into arriving clotheslined sphere,
tucks,
explodes up-field
cornerback-linebacker-safety pursued
exotic coordination
of brain-muscle-blood
impeccably blueprinted, milled
to thousandth centimeter
maximum lung productivity
pumping pumping
beautifully
49 yard line
37
18
dodges tackle
squiggles
dodges another
9
3
two in-diving tacklers like bottlenose dolphins,
elongated, arms outstretched
ellipses in magnificent fingers
fully attenuated,
dives for corner
crossing plane
by half inch
as blind-siders plow him over,
skid on pads, faceguard, chin, butt
to heroic halt
on tartan track,

explosion of immortality
in Lucas Oil Stadium
as quarterback slams him
chest-to-chest crashing upward sea spume bliss
Super Bowl lead and winning score
post-game 50-yard line jubilation
And MVP designation
As lips kiss blinding erection,
eyes lifted toward God.

*I*RVING FRYING reds, bait shrimp in cottage's faded
kitchen, Eddie, proud angler, bragging of catch,
"Sister", "Nookie" nude under moo-moos, brown
creamy gams, kids dashing full of crushes and
Vinton, "Who's ready!" shouts chef over pan-hissing,
spatula prying flesh—blackened, sticking—plastic
flatware, grocery store ice, Bonneville wagon,
fish-slimy outboard on oyster shell drive, distant
combers crashing, Texas heat pressing breasts,
flattening coifs, night descending in blanket of
crickets house beats back with crackling florescence,
laughter, lewd quips, room dancing with Jewish
ancestry—Vexler's Slovenia, Massman's Alsace—
and the thrill of future prosperity—Panama, Alaska,
"Viva Merida!" But tonight rabble fish, iceberg,
butter, baguettes, Neapolitan wedges, men in
jump suits, chipped sink, funky wall dress, blur
of voices, fly strip, kids streaming round furniture
legs, rotten frame house plus rancid outbuilding
crammed with buggy bunks where the babies
sleep between ridiculous and real, Harold, Shep
snore on screen porch, Irving, Ed with wives get
bedrooms—past and future crush fuck out people,
snapshots ease the grip, here's one of Ed beam-
ing with pride, a fat bull-red sagging between fists.

*I*N HIS FINAL incoherent muttering hours I believe my father experienced gladness. *Enough pills, bowel movements, shoes, TV. Enough news and asinine children. Relief, finally, to lie in a room removed from life's beet grater. Lament not my demise.* I believe one sumptuous word freighted every drool-pearl: peace, ease, repose, freedom, worldly matters besieged me—home renovation, inspection sticker, storm door replacement, driveway erosion, as, dashing about, I displaced whirlwinds of air. *You never understood,* I hear him confess, *how torturous it was to prepare each morning my gladiator face. Competition massacred like leaf cutter ants.* Night revealed all. *Hell over, I've put down my mask which resembles, you see, an iron furnace grate. What freshness nakedness is! I was never sublime or brilliant, destined to blaze, I scudded across trashy warehouse floor dead machines stocked with garbage for nickels and dimes—a dumb brutish enterprise for mortgage and meals. Failure and deception shaved my principles to raw splintered bone. Now I lie protected from the dense teeming horror where even traffic is somatic. Grieve not my passing for I am bliss. Stop touching me. Go away. Take, my children, your insincere faces back to Boston and Houston and stop fussing over me. You—not I—are the tragedy. The sooner you stop pretending to love me the sooner your release from this charade which lacerated me and from which my death is joyful deliverance.*

DEATH FRENCH kisses, plunges tongue like a dagger.
Orgasms carpet spine.

Addiction seizes brain.

Death-nicotine.

Death slithers all one's orifices,

Like a many-bodied snake,

Inseminating everything simultaneously.

One awakes in cold clenched embrace,

Tongue thrusting gut,

Syrupy endearments

Layering pulse.

Alone one sleeps, coital one blinks.

Up for cereal and fruit.

Terrycloth slippers. Banging kitchen.

Vagina sore. Bowlegged hobble.

Pulling winter through door to meet buddy

For mustard.

Dull murmur.

Death mugs love with bone billy club

Like a Casanova *Schutzstaffel*.

And mothers birth ashes, maggots, oyster shell, nail.

One births kohlrabi,

Tree bark, window pane dagger.

It's the time for magical packages—wrapping paper, bows.

One for little Georgie, one for Danielle.

Toy backhoe, stuffed Snuffleupagus.

Who could've known?

One for grandma: shawl for chilly facility.

Death opens mouth, French kisses like ripper.

Beautiful. Luxurious. Glinty as silver.

I love death's muscled clean scaly flesh.

I love its sweet meticulousness.

Its scrupulousness.

Death the dependable framer
With nail gun and level.
Its horologist's quibble.
Give peace, O Tannenbaum.
Give indemnification.
It pins one to bed, pries lips, tongue into stomach while body
      down nostrils, vagina, ears, ass hole coming over roe.
Carried two years to term she delivers
Tumor, lizard, gristle, crematoria.

*I* SLEEP ON bed pushed against two walls—one veneer, one
brick—down hall first door right. Here, sixty years ago I rolled
head to Vanilla Fudge, Keep Me Hanging On, exhilarated. I
lie now in that same air space, house empty, mother dead,
and I home to stand watch on daddy in hospital dying.
Predictable paradigm. Adult child parenting helpless adult.
Diaper, feeding, dressing, delivering. Bizarre. Everywhere
parents battle children. Raw family antagonism. Now finally
quietude. Muffin in slippers appears in kitchen where I am
having oatmeal. She is pasty, emaciated, forehead jutting
out thinning hair. Her flax a bowel constitutional. We
will dress, go to him—Rick already there—stand vigil. But
now glide through private sanctuaries—his, hers, pink
tile bath. Both parents had superior dentals. Remember
when she murdered Feathers? Here against cabinetry,
obeying taboo against striking one's parent, in frustration
and anger I fused two knuckles. Wander the formal dining
room aglitter with heirlooms—crystal, silver, portraits,
linen. Laughter of Seders—exploded glass slivers—stuck in
wall paper. That infernal croaking pantry, still not repaired.
Somewhere a safe lies under terrazzo. I glide in chocolate
Sorel slippers down hall first door right. He is waiting.

*Y*OU READING THIS—
Fuck off.

Think I care
About you?

Fuck yourself.
You're dead

Soon, too,
Another failed cricket

Decomposing
Somewhere.

Because I'm you
I despise you.

Revolving sphere
Plows up continuous

Mornings
Like carpet bombs.

We're all contemptible.
I hate you

Your obsequiousness,
Ineptitude.

Not one of us
But marches off

Naked, wrists lashed,
Smeared with spit

And excrement,
Worthless

As we have lived
Inside bombast,

Pomposity,
Buried by

Megalomania.
Because I crave immortality—

God envy—
And cannot achieve it

I hate and suggest
You fuck off.

I make a fist to bash
What's not physical—

Conqueror, waste-layer—
But collapse in chair,

As I did at my mother's
Dirt bed.

I couldn't save her.
Instead cried "mommy,"

The short pants kid.
I detest you.

What isn't stupidity
Is lunacy,

What isn't lunacy
Absurdity.

All man has is erectility,
Or memory of it.

*I* REFRAIN FROM demonic hysterics,
From spewing like glass guttural laughter.
It would look like exorcism.
I do not flinch, reveal no inclination.
Suavely with friends I parry conversation, legs intellectually knee-crossed.
I assent and contribute, sip wine, am fetching.
Something inside rips asylum of flesh.
Convulsive rage.
I restrain raw aggression.
Rage of impermanence, rage of helplessness,
Rage of imperfection
Against implacable monster.
I am a packed functioning organism death can burst like clod between fingers.
I contain myself but knowledge hurts. I am not mine to keep.
My hands look pathetic, disconnected, apish.
I suppress acid.
I freeze bullet a millisecond before window.
Window behind window awaiting explosion.
Were humans but porcelain. Were man just synthetic.
I live in continuous shuddering pre-shatter.
Dining, for instance, with glittering crystal
Or reading by fire.
Sometimes I just must leave the table.
Sometimes I require blood on the napkin.
Recently illness has thinned me to tissue through which pain bleeds.
Inner ear condition.
Rage loves the wrecked package.
I am sixty-three, married, grandfather twice,
And live comfortably in the Berkshires
Near museum, theater.
At finales I stand, applaud, shout bravo.
I harness intensity in service of roundness.
Disclosure such as this satiates the griffon.

Art requires sanity.
I shall rejoin now downstairs knitting
By the fire my partner
From whose life I quietly departed.

"*I*HAD GOT her pregnant so what could I do? Question of honor. Her daddy asked if I love her: trapped, a typical youth ill-equipped at self-loyalty, so I lied. I didn't love her but weight of responsibility and pressure of living fetus crushed me in guilt; I loved another. I attempted to break it off, repeatedly, but capitulated under tearful histrionics, and, weakened once again, slipped between thighs. Sperm worked egg. So there I sat with her parents to announce their happy grand-parentage. I agreed to elope to Travis County Courthouse like enhanced romantics. Though I cried before entering with cash in wallet and freedom at curb, I suffered in and fulfilled obligation, wrecking my world. Afterward we had Surf & Turf at Lamplighter Inn and shattered champagne on Paradise's hull. Emotionally misshapen, squeezed to uncharacteristic personal contortion: rage, adultery, ridicule, indifference, I drove wife and zygote through a series of junky syphilitic towns into the heart of mediocrity. This too, of course, is a rhapsody of death."

*I*F NOT FOR it eternal happiness
If not for it cake cake and cake
If not for it endless engorgement
If not for it unblemished comprehension
If not for it infinite chariots
If not for it universal virtuosity
If not for it impish mischief-making
If not for it fearlessness
If not for it anti-festschrifts
If not for it keen olfactory kill
If not for it mesmeric chimera
If not for it raw totalitarianism
If not for it celestial velvet cape
If not for it sparkling red viscera
If not for it plowed-under savagery, buried guilt
If not for it perpetual shattering flattery
If not for it life's emulsifier eternally eaten by acid's cynicism
If not for it immemorial acts of cruelty, tenderness, indifference
If not for it numberless holocausts
If not for it vanishing viper swallowing its own self-regenerating tail
    of perseverance and triumph in an endless cycle of repeating
    reappearances
If not for it continuous performance of perfidious compulsions
If not for it incalculable occasions for superior oratory
If not for it indomitable rhinoceros-plated Tang warrior-prince at bat-
    tle-clash ravaging adversaries with pike of righteousness, hammer
    of rage
If not for it bird chatter sanctity
If not for it glory of humility
If not for it rhapsodic relief
If not for it Mustang, Sting Ray, GTO spine-tingling drag race grudge
    match forever
If not for it unremitting torment of monotony, monomania

If not for it decomposition of rationality into comforting infantile fairy
    tale

If not for it fiendish addiction to purification of soul

If not for it untold riches

If not for it saag paneer, lamb Tandoori, rosewater pudding everlasting

If not for it spooning abed with my baby incorruptible

If not for it pastoralism, tranquility, serenity imperishable

*Baa, baa, black sheep,*

*Have you any wool?*

*Yes sir, yes sir,*

*Three bags full*

How do you say goodbye to utility knife, beach glass, animal crackers,
    sand?

How do you say goodbye to great blue heron?

How do you say goodbye to Tom Dorsey, Cab Calloway?

How do you say goodbye to cotton shirt falling over skin?

How do you say goodbye to slatted chair, murmuring aroma?

How do you say goodbye to green peepers breaking black humus?

How do you say goodbye to timbre, tone, color, pitch?

How do you say goodbye to worn-smooth gold-plate heirloom wrist-
    watch?

How do you say goodbye to politics, aesthetics, hypothesis, postulation?

How do you say goodbye to intuition, instinct, achievement, character?

How do you say goodbye to corner's familiar chipped edges?

How do you say goodbye to sea turtle baby?

How do you say goodbye to "mum's 4 sale" roadside placard?

How do you say goodbye to mustard yellow vase, porcelain elephant,
    concrete gargoyle, lighthouse key holder?

How do you say goodbye to sighing branches?

How do you say goodbye to dry British novels, wet Brazilian verse?

How do you say goodbye to beaded balsa gecko?

How do say goodbye to reminiscence, dream, blackberry, warmth?

How do you say goodbye to gold lame bed skirt?

How do you say goodbye to hammer, pliers, wrench, cliff?

How do you say goodbye to ranch style, craftsman, gambrel,
revival, old colonial, bungalow, Cotswold, foursquare,
desert modern, neo-classical, tidewater, straw bale, stucco,
hovel, rat trap, plain Jane, nondescript, fifties track, prefab,
module, duplex, apartment full of cats, hamsters, shadows,
doubles, inflections, textures, thrill, cream-filled cake?

How do you say goodbye to newspaper morning cup presiden-
tial race between horrible and great, everything at risk:
healthcare, minimum wage, corporate control, economy,
regulation, stability of middle class, Medicaid and Medi-
care, Democracy itself climbing up spine, through brain,
down legs, saturating rind in this most critical, requiring,
soul-demanding, get-out-vote election in history of world?

How do you say goodbye to Mud Pie, Double Trouble, Black Ti-
ger, Kahlua Sombrero, Three Geeks and Red Head, Moose
Trail, Bada Bing in one big puff-release into flaccidity and
inanimation?

How do you say goodbye to nasty nor'easter sheeting across
sky, breeching land, slamming into face like a slap of
skin-bracer zinging blood and electrifying brain into sting-
ing vivacity?

How do you say goodbye to gravitron, rock-o-plane, octopus,
tilt-a-whirl?

How do you say goodbye to panic attack, obsession, paranoia,
obesity, mother's ratty slippers, delicate spider web,
self-flagellation, mediocrity, clumsiness, aching knees,
Metamucil, weightless flitter, failure, above all failure—
spiritually, professionally, artistically, psychologically—
which gives piquancy and value to anonymous existence?

How do you say goodbye to

How do you say goodbye to

How do you say goodbye to limeade, lymphoma, toxic waste,

Anita Ekberg, echocardiographic woof, voiceless echo, intuitive
projection, dromedary cud-chewing, Paradise bar, Gary Larsen,
staked tomatoes, engine purr, tomorrow's disaster, foolproof
diet, wooden ships—volunteers—had to cry today—cry baby—
black napkins—southern man—with a little help—light my
fire—fresh garbage—star spangled—stairway heaven—going
home—I'm glad—spoonful—memory Elizabeth Reed—Euro-
pa—oh god the songs, the wonderful songs, the looping, long,
drugged-out, transformational, gut-ripping rhapsodies to anger,
outrage, resistance, resurrection—Ohio?

If not for it corrections toward restitution for infelicities committed
toward a conversation with perfection,

How do you say goodbye to table, bowl, distance, water?

All the power of the world cuts off.

"OOH," "OW," "OH," face squinched like lemon-suck as attendant adjusts him. Arthritis perhaps, jagged edges. I'm not dying. Muffin's not. He's dying. His turn. I know what's killing him. His vitals test negative. Gibberish dribbles. Diaper swells with urine. "Ooh," "Ooh," "Ow," lemon face, recoil. Eyes pinched. The room is fine. View of lawn, local traffic. Nurses kind but have their demons. And that progressive pain chart. The white board says "Thursday". I never touched him and do not now. Ice. Muffin strokes his face. I wander foyer. Dead mother expunged him decades ago, his receded penis needed plunging. In her final days she refused his presence. Now he dies. Neither edematous nor palsied. She wanted to die last, imagined hemlock. Some women are born sexless, porcelain. We ate off pink Formica. When young buddies and I played war with Wham-O, chinaberries. Noldan put out Moeller's eye. Ammunition grew in my yard. Fifty years ago. This is serious. I doubt she ever loved him.

*I*T'S NOTHING," HE says, "I'm fine, just a little setback."
Perhaps he's right. He's not. My sister has driven
from Houston, I have flown from Boston. His nurse
is tired, fatalistic. "Rick," Daddy says, "hold
tight." "Where're we going? Where's Roslyne?"
(She's dead.) His pants fall off. He can't work
zippers. "Where're we eating?" We get him in
the car. "It's just a whatchamacallit?" "Recurrence,"
we say. "It'll be fine." (He's right. The cancer
doesn't kill him.) I'm the driver. My sister shotgun.
Daddy in back with Rick. We're motionless on
the driveway. "Where're we eating?" The house
is left, red brick ranch rimmed with dead
grass. Gray trim, peeling. A green lizard cocks
head. It's eight AM, we're off to chemo. I'll
take Santa Fe to Doddridge to Ocean Dr. I
want to see water. Nobody cares. Across the
street at Dunham's a lawn crew sets up. Touch
brakes, press button. (I haven't yet.) Seat
belt crosses chest, green, like the CTS. The
double garage gapes. In school after night of
boozing I growled up this drive in my 327, shut
it down with a rattle. Ate hemis. Now I sit
in fatuous sedan sixty years later with an old
woman, a middle age nurse, a yammering cadaver.
It's already boiling, cicadas clacking. Where're
the natal plum bushes? I used to fry monarch
pupas. My sister looks task oriented, adamant,
chewing lip. I've gotten fat. I suppose, I think,
but don't know what follows. I just suppose.
"Is everybody buckled?" "Daddy?" "Let's go to
the Mason Jar." I have not yet pushed the button.

*I* 'M SICK OF death, sick of thinking about it, sick of writing about it, sick of obsessing about it, sick of the MGM Grand/Ziegfried Follies/Cecil B. DeMille/ Ten Commandments of it, sick of the Super Bowl half-time spectacle of it, sick of its spider-finger precision and hunger-inevitability, sick of homicide and suicide ideations, nightmare death dreams, putty tooth horror dreams, plane crash dreams, sick of poison-pestilence-influenza-streptococcus-monoxide gas-staff occupation, sick of melancholia-dyspepsia-neurasthenia-lugubriousness-gloom-iness-apathy-ennui, nauseated by its botulism, diarrheic with its spoilage, re-fluxed by its taint, sick of the Hindenburg Zeppelin-fifty megaton combustion of it, sick of the soul rot-brain mold-penis canker of it, sick of the knee scrape-ankle break-herniated disk of it, sick of punch-holing real people, exhausted by dance marathon-hypothalamus screaming, eternal electioneering rabidity, sick of its spectacle glass-scratch, sick of its bitter coffee, sick of dog shit littered yard.

I want to live, I want to pulse, I want to enjoy, I want to savor, taste, I want to floor it and heave torque, I want to cut glass with facet, I want to steal Starry Night, I want to shoot come on dandelion stalk, I want salt encrusted rope, I want to fire a night-gun at God while stoned on hashish, I want to vote for Jimmy Durante, Red Skelton, Jack Benny, Pinky Lee, I want to stretch lips over head and eat myself to feet, I want little flower bombs of psychoanalysis exploding across ass, I want hair and teeth and knees and fingerprints, I want love so deep I sleep under her liver, I want live sewer frogs peeking out fist, I want Victor Victrola, Betty Boop Pez, Black Cow Caramel, I want immortality in showering spume, I want to hear Walt Disney Fess Parker Davy Crockett theme song come to rest on a fresh episode, buckskin fringe, black powder musket, forged steel Bowie, I want to suck down thin frigid air and exhale over world like Edmund Hillary, I want to press courage-poultice and amulet gel into my cripple that I may walk to garden from chair.

I'm healthy, hearty, hungry, hale, I'm corpuscle bilirubin rich, red and white caplets hop-scotch my blood, I'm muscular with pink tip, I have toes like sea mussels and hair like Pibb fizz, I'm greased in BP and lubed in Pennzoil, I bend disks like segmented fish and over Lex Luthor lock glistening victory pecs, I'm soft-bodied sissy dripping vanilla ripe for slaughter, I'm squid of happiness with bones of lace, *papier mache* veins, see me sleet on cowardice's paste precipice, I paint like a piston huge bosomed nudes demure as bashful bombs with oils made of Eden's ground ocean pearls, I'm heat magmatic of life surcease, see me reverse Earth's magnetic whirl like Christopher Reeves in cherry silk boots, I'm happenstance in tweed wielding Popeye fists and encyclopedic wit born on July first like a thrown sun pulse, I'm vital, elemental, sturdy, crisp and I'm sick of fear, I'm sick of death, I'm sick of dread and tyrannical doom, I'm sick of chloroform and drop-kicked head, I'm sick of plumb-bob dragging down lids, let contemplative human brain fucking itself in a bin with self-referential horror glare, let me burrow moist loam and not poke to blink at orb's super-dizzying gyroscope, I'm uninterested in baptism and ecumenical cleansing, I want to be thick with leaf milk and chlorophyll's singular mission, happy in weather, a monolith, sick of atrophy of hatchet-awareness, sick of cemeteries, obituaries, milestone passages, morbidity, lamination, and liquid intelligence, death is everything: the coffee boutique tete-a-tete, the football victory, new paint, the Martinique vacation, Ouija at Pat's, vichyssoise and nicoise, nurturing human warmth. I'm busting out Leavenworth, my homemade iron maiden, jumping into diapers and toddling through December focused and clapping, heart reattached like a blurry whirling pupil, I'm ginger ale and bran buds and tablet of antacid, I'm application and absorption and splattered white smock, I'm permission and radiation and racks of bric-a-brac, see me in dilation, intakes flapped open, ship funnels blowing, see me in ecstasy, stunned as a prawn, unwound, unplugged, rotund on chair, I don't care, I don't matter, nothing requires action, two vicious kidneys eat each other in corner, I'm beyond, I'm indifferent, it's irrelevant, it's finished, two toothsome monsters sink in boiling gore, Gordon's through with torture.

*I*N DRESS SHOES and boxers, fists bared, belligerent-daddy rushes me composed in chair charging *totalitarian, fascist, SS man.* He sprays spit. Go ahead, punch me. Murderous intent. Always wanted to crush me. My lifestyle rankles. Decades earlier, raging at his butch-waxed slacker, bullied me into a corner threatening a lesson. Failure gnawed him. Married to a Frigidaire. Hoarfrost lips. Cold glinting lacquer. The monstrous children. All that megalomania, frustration, bitterness gibberish now on death-bed, toes spearing sheet. Whirling magneto expending last wattage. Pasty. Heaving. I recall him in his glory charging field after slaughtering yolk, whetted on fantasies of triumph, celebration, inestimable warrior. Here lies result, ravaged unadulterated failure. I have a god with picked head sores, deflated shapeless nipples, bloodless sagging ass, lipless, thundering down sky to rape no Leda, representing his species. I ask nothing less. Like a man fearing dead rattler, I cannot touch him. He might strike yet. I keep distance issuing uncomfortable phrases, *We're here beside you, we love you...great father...fearless warrior...restored to blossom mom is waiting... will always cherish...you are a wonderful man,* and to myself I add, *and such a tragedy.*

*R*ICK GIVES HIM a year without Roslyne.
Look at him, he says, pathetic.
Rick says he's seen this before,
How surviving mate wastes.
My sister says "too mean to die".
Says she could kill him.
I wish she would.
This is Cat on Hot Tin.
Everybody wants Big Daddy dead,
Big Brutal Daddy.
Daddy doesn't know night from day, where he is.
Daddy doesn't remember Roslyne's dead, sobs each time we tell him.
"She's dead," we say, "remember?"
"God Almighty," head in tears.
"When's the funeral?"
I fantasize piercing eyes with needles.
God knows what Muffin wishes.
I imagine de-throating him.
It's impressive the revulsion this man's aroused.
On her deathbed his "beautiful" wife
Refused his touch.
He floated behind grievers as she died.
A driving cap smashed his head.
Anyway, Rick says won't last a year.
Nine months, tops, he says.
Daddy invents a myth.
"We had story book marriage,
Epic love."
(She stiffened at his every approach.)
"Made in heaven."
He deteriorates like a banana.
Grows slimy, rancid.
Trails shit on carpet.

Weeps all night

Driving Rick mad with sleeplessness.

Only Rick loves him,

Grew to love him.

Rick says my father has regrets

Too proud to admit.

Rick phones. He's dying.

I travel two thousand miles.

I, too, have regrets, but more predominantly acid.

I sniffle but Rick sobs. I am losing lousy father, Rick good friend.

He does not die open-jawed like mother.

His death is tranquil.

He just goes to sleep.

*A* SWATH OF mother's concrete grave liner
Peeks into daddy's fresh gouged plot.
Peering down I see the piece.
Law requires solid walls encase cadavers
To prevent groundwater contamination
In this coastal town where
They lived seventy years in
Love and bitterness.
Just as daddy crashed her peace,
He now crashes her decomposition.
Her rotting face falls in disbelief.
Enter badgering pugilist.
I smirk at such bitter enemies eternally
Buried hip to hip
And memorialized on one headstone
As enviable lovers.
Ironic protocol.
Death's industry prettifies.
All their dead friends populate Seaside Memorial:
The Jerome Nasts,
The Jerry Birnbergs,
The Paul Racusins,
The Hyman Goodmans and tragic Sandra,
The Hymie Roosths,
Rabbi Sydney and Bebe Wolf,
Harry Samuels and young Brad,
Sylvan Wolfson and child Stevie,
Julius Rosenberg.
Now the Edward Massmans,
Last to arrive.
Perhaps underground they slap down whist hands.
I return to Plainfield, Massachusetts, to wife, friends:
Alice & Susan,

Bob & June,

Allen & Anne,

Jim & Judy,

Laurie & Elaine,

Helene

Dave & Bette

Ed & Anne

With whom I share repast,

Politics,

Philosophy,

Tears,

Cheer,

Civic duty,

Charades,

Succor,

Or, as now, the board game Aggravation

Played at table with die and pieces

To magic and laughter.

I stare into their faces.

*M*Y FATHER'S LIFE flashes.

Dying eyelids flutter.

Cut glass decanter.

Rainbow on ceiling.

Bed wetting. Bed. Mommy castigating.

Tin pump carousel.

Knickers.

Afraid.

Orange balloon. Goodbye string.

Loneliness.

Football. Louisiana sweat. Dirty pigskin.

Daddy. Big head. Ships. Alone. Mom angry.

Beaumont.

Boxing. Brown gloves. Blood. Filth. Glory.

Fraternity. Frat boy. Upper class. Marketing. Engineering. Precision.
Perfectionism.

Daddy's letter: Business! Not profession. Business!

Dead. Dead. Oh god. Daddy.

Boxing. Guts. Dirty. Work. Work and soldiering. Grunt. Push. Shove.
Prevail.

Collapse. Zap. Zap. Zap. Zap. Weep. Electricity. Weep. Rock on toilet.

Destitution. Heart attack. Failure. Push. Push. Demand. Urge. Acid.
Tums.

So beautiful. Cruel. I didn't mean. Punishment. Cold. Banished. Alone.

Pills. Pills. Pills. Pills. Son. Daughter. Tiny. Ignorant.

Idiots.

Shame. Public shame. No. Never. No forgiveness. Borrow. Loan. Steal.
Lie.

Prop up. Bolster. Why? Why did I? Broken head. Immoral. Weak. Don't
know.

Don't know. No warmth. No skin. No touch. Never. Never more. Con-
victed.

Convict. Breakdown. Pills. Pills. Pills. Pills. Hospital. Blow over. For-

118

give. Letter. Please.

Swagger. Rubdown. Manicure. Talcum. Pima night clothes.

Unfulfilled. Delusion. Monster. Queen. Sheba queen.

Sell. Start over. New idea. Big. Big money. Reconciliation. Love. High
    profits.

Fools. Fools. All fools. I, champion. I, savior. I, superman.

Watch me go. Ding dong daddy, Dumas.

Do ma stuff.

Unstoppable.

Top of heap.

Mr. Sublimity. Coup de grace. Not my fault. I didn't. He just. Wasn't.
    Don't blame. Chosen. By God. To excel.

Kids. Kids. Kids. Migrating cheeky heel-dragging insensitive hot-stuff
    disobedient aliens. Greed-stalks. I can't. It's. How could. I mean.
    God almighty. Impossible.

Hustle.

Crisis.

Empty.

Nothing.

Mr. Universe. Invincible. Pills. Pills. Pills. Bed-torture. Night-hell. Pris-
    on. Disgrace. Must happen.

She, love, executed, lost, gone, if I, television, divorce, but love love,
    what happened, why, snarl, hates me, dead, irrecoverable. Suicide.

Skid. Paris. Mazatlan. Whales. Somewhere before. When we were. Bo-
    soms. Legs. Nail paint. Muscles. Before. And the babies. The beach.
    Oh. The sea. Flounder. Speckleds. Drum. Bull Reds. Firm croaking
    jewel-flicking flesh. Rod resisting. Red Garcia Abumatic.

Goldberg, Frank, Sharlock, and that woman Vexler.

Should have been. More. Well, they'll just. Virtue of forgiveness. Who
    are they?

Now this. Shit. Longitude and latitude of it. Implacable immensity
Inescapable. Dust. Dust. Well. At least. Reunited What was? Where was?
    Where am? Who? Can't. Naked? Ooh! Ooh! hurts! Don't! Okay.

I'm. Okay. Ready. I'm. I'm. Desperate gills. Flopping. Fiberglass.
Echo.

But this shitty. Chest. Pain. Sore. Space. Letting grip. Fingers
blossoming. Don't want.

This. Stubborn. Interminable. Squirting. Grape seed.

(Last night, 3:00 AM, no answer, peacefully, please, yes, of course,
naturally.)

*D*ADDY'S SISTER arrives for the funeral.

Her son, Robert, 61, drives her from Houston.

She lives on two planets.

Her dead husband sweats in yard.

Her father sends letters.

She doesn't know me.

She thinks my sister is her granddaughter.

The funeral is sparsely attended.

The Rabbi is generous:

Good Husband.

Good father.

Past Temple President.

Perfect attendance.

Civic minded.

Tenacious businessman.

Devout angler.

Philanthropist.

My sister and I taste irony's rust.

My father's sister is flummoxed.

"Who's dead?"

"We in Beaumont?"

"Corpus Christi," we correct.

"Your brother passed."

"Edwin?"

"Not Edwin. Edward. Edward died."

Oh.

I adore my aunt.

She's guileless.

Her older son, Allan, 65, reveals her sadism.

Gloried in his anal worms.

He's a shrink in New Bedford.

We have a graveside service.

Two straps undergird the coffin

Which floats above the gash.
After Kaddish taut young attendants
Crank him down.
They are elsewhere.
Fucking, perhaps.
Smoking crack.
The aged faces of past acquaintances shock me.
"None other than!" "It is I!"
Scott brokers insurance.
Robert's an otolaryngologist.
A sudden infarction killed Brownstein.
We noodle.
One palms his business card.
To my sister: "They're together again."
"Poor Mom," she weeps.
Seaside Memorial.
We climb into limo.
Ride to cars.
My sister clutches daddy's flag.
He typed in Philly, WW2.
I covet it but sister's adamant.
I'm always compliant.
Now it's logic:
The furniture.
The house.
The Cadillac.
The crap.
Dense as a brick.
Fifty eight years thick.
They're in the paint.
We're not blubbering as with mother.
We're cold and want to get on with it.
To dealer we sell the Fleetwood.

Split the check.

With Re/Max we list the house.

The furniture tosses about me like salad leaves.

We have no reception.

My father's sister sits blankly.

Smiling.

Senility blunts bereavement.

I'm skidding on slammed brakes.

My feelings, hitting tree, fly through windshield.

I stare at my sister.

I stare at cousins.

I know not what to feel.

This is about me.

I'm shifted, shifting.

The dead irrelevant.

It's my story.

My father's sister rises, wanders. Where's the bedroom?

They pile back into the car. Disappear.

What now?

My sister's husband is expertly repressed.

Overwhelming variables numb my sister.

I'm tired.

She's tired.

Her husband types on laptop.

Everyone has dispersed.

Earth digests both parents.

The furniture gapes.

Ghosts.

Realtor brings an offer.

We close.

We transfer keys.

I rock in my chair home in Plainfield,

Read **Bury My Face At Wounded Knee.**

This is not metaphorical.
No one massacred my parents.
It's just what I'm reading.
I pillow-prop the book on lap.
I underline unfamiliar words like "wickiup" and "ambuscade"
And star outrageous passages.
The pillow serves as a desk.
What can one do?
I made resolutions I failed to keep,
grounded in idealism.
The heart drops into its slot.
Old photos climb up my sister like stegosaurus plates: Grandma, Nana
Papa, baby shots, studio portraits, birthday albumettes.
Photographs bury her.
I'm on the toilet squeezing out blood.

# PART III

**B**LOOD! BLOOD! BLOOD! We want blood!
Jaguars! Redskins! Dolphins! Rams!
Slaughter! Murder! Send 'em to morgue!
Kill the wabbit! Kill the wabbit!
Stomp 'em in ground! Fist pump. Chest thump.
Kick 'em in the groin! Smash mouth!
Smash mouth! Roar lion roar.
Knock 'em down, roll 'em round!
Fight Crusaders Fight!
Vikings! Titans! Bengals! Browns!
Knife 'em in the eye! Kill the wabbit!
Kill the wabbit! Blow to kingdom come!
Nuclear roar. War roar. Bowl bowl bowl.
One collective bared locked flex.
Shotgun! Blitz! Bomb! Flack!
Crowd explodes! String 'em high!
Crucify! Hang the bums!
One rock hard purple cock,
One wet tight cunt. Hang niggers!
Gas Jews! Bash! Bash! Burn!
Castrate filthy sicko queers,
Cram it in their bum.
Rock you! Rock you! Gonna fuckin' rock!
Bash heads! Crack bones!
Shatter 'em in the nuts!
Blow 'em away! Strike 'em dead.
March on to V-I-C-T-O-R-Y!
Drown all kikes in briny sea!
Hail Victors! Hail to Thee!
We're the mighty Green!
Slaughter 'em! Scalp 'em!
Unravel 'em on a chain
Down the rocky lane!

Eat spleen! Eat gut!

Eat raw livers three.

Leave 'em on battlefield blown smithereens!

One eye there, one ear here.

One arm in tree!

Eagles! Packers! Panthers! Bears!

Rapists! Sadists! Glee!

Char the sodomists! Skewer perverts!

Pop darkies on spit!

Black Knight fans, clap your hands,

Mash 'em into glue!

Who are you, who are we,

We're the Red and Blue!

These boots were made for walkin', Buster,

Wildcats take control!

Spike shoulders, bone necklace, fanged grotesque skull.

Solid grease blue naked gut tatted with a "D",

"D" for death! Death! Death!

Death! Death! Death! Kill

The wabbit! Kill the wabbit!

Plunge arms in boiling gore!

Plunge arms in hot entrails!

*T*HEY ARE WHORES, we eat crap, drink incessantly, rarely bathe, abort babies, live in filth—needles, wrappers, cigarette butts—tricks for blow, steal and sell, mug, crash in pits, shoot in lavatories, get fucked up, hate, love, ball guts, we disappointed but you deserved, we score food stamps, stuff steak down pants, not always fucked, crash in rehab, clean up, resolution, never sticks, backslide, want conventionality but are trash, statistic, underbelly spunk flooding street, but it's a blast, they are whores, we are whores, when you've got nothing else you've got your holes, you're always worth something, some- one's always buying, euphoria crawling spine, wrapping brain, knocking you dead light years from dullards, stiffs, divorce, rage, but blame ourselves and ache for rest, regress childlike— swing set, slide—regret, yes, moment of divergence, like what Billy Kid might have felt while being drilled, we veered wrong and grew small, shouting farewell, and disappeared, for years you bargained, clutched, shelled out, finally resigned like pinioned bugs, they are whores, needles dirty, winters cold, we are always constipated, diarrheic, we are contemptible pestilential rats, dead jellies sliming life, we are adults with wiry crotches, reeking flesh, semen strings and sheets of grunge, but they are whores, seedy, cheap, worthless bums and we whoremongers, scum.

*D*EALER SELLS CRACK to junkie on credit.
It's nothing to dispose of meat, he says.
Stuff it in dumpster.
Another dead bum.
Cops got bigger problems.
Think they care?
Don't deliver, die.
I've got associates.
No mercy.
They've begged, bargained, prayed—
Worthless.
Money's it. Period.
Do I look like Mother Theresa?
By five, fucker. Eight-hundred fifty.
Don't care, just get it.
Nothing to me but meal ticket.
Cash or flesh.
Peel it or bite it.
Not pretty:
Struggle, thrust, unconscious, dead.
One gets used to food,
Shelter,
Clothing,
Wheels.
What pity.
Crying shame.
I'm Ramses, you're Jew.
Build a pyramid.
Pathetic asshole.
They love to kill, gorillas. Methods.
Impressive methods.
They'll never find you.
Okay. I'm decent.

Tomorrow, three.
Don't screw me.
I'll be waiting.
I'm your best friend.
Bro.
Don't tempt my goons.
They eat losers like flour.

*I*S VIGOR AND health: half-gainer, jackknife, trampoline, tennis

Is bammin' 'n slammin': garter, V-string, condom, cock ring

Is shakin' 'n bakin': contract, commission, acquisition, promotion

Is makin' bacon: baby, family, episiotomy, whipping

Is abstract and genius and vision and tenacity

Is booming and looming: vice-president, pin stripe, Mont Blanc, satchel

Is six pack and rugby and Guinness and discretion

Is ruddiness

Is buttock-flex

Is utility knife

Is brilliance

Is animal sacrifice, crossbow

Is ram fuel induction

Is molding, twisting, smearing her fascia

Is volcanically erupting

Is island sun sinking into ocean between legs propped on railing, big
    bloody egg

Is top of hub: Egyptian, Alpaca, grand complication

Is green hi-top All Stars, contractor chinos, conductor, mallard duck
    clacker

Is men's silver bracelet

Is cookin' and smokin': puncher, ranch land, sheepskin, Great Pyrenees

Is Whistler, Killington, lung pump, thigh action

Is touchdown electrification

Is spontaneous wit, improvisational lip

Is knocking down pins: takeover, merger, bloodbath, dismissal

Is smooth as water: Maserati, Gulf Stream, jai alai, Johnny Walker

Is queen of scene: sweeping, gracious, magisterial, lethal

Is absenteeism, indifference

Is hammock between beeches

Is infinity pool on Cabo San Lucas

Is hipsterism

Is *Concours d'elegance*

Is delicious hedonistic nihilism

Is cymbal clash in tree meat

Is tenacity of conviction

Is skin elasticity

Is virile burr haircut

Is eggs Florentine fertility

Is shuddering oscillating frothing hot plasma

Is *e to the –y power minus e to the y power over 2i equals 1e to the y power minus e to the –y power over i2 equals 1 sinh(y)*

Is snap tongue, flash eye, smack thumb, slap drum

Is incontrovertible certainty in canary convertible

Is big-horn sure-hoof picking rock precipice

Is hostess with mostest: pork roast, warm dressing, zoom rocket tits

Is monogramed haberdashery, cat's eye cuff link

Is Johnny on spot: sucking rattler venom, rifle-flipping Gila, stitching brow gash, bow-drilling fire

Is vigorous self-image crackling through pupil

Is not *fait accompli*

Is not down for count bony-hipped big-skull coughing up liver on shit-spotted sheet amidst nightmare machines croaking out vitals, an apocalyptic frog opera

Is not lost it lymphomatous babble-drivel spasm-brain clothes hanger bony on institutional mattress like a rheumatoid grasshopper, all coccyx and scapula, jaw joint rictus like water-eroded granite, sweat-eye in fear and hellish regret of losing loss lost, bailing extraneous fat-phlegm-acid-hair like flotsam from skiff, all pathos and bewilderment, flummox and hate, excision and bitterness

Is not dry-spittle crust-eye foot-in-grave cabbage punching morphine button like video game slaughter, pain yelper, pain nipper sliding down razor, horrific, horrific, claws sunk in brain clay, terra cotta hell, smiley face showering sour lemon tears onto waxed institutional squares, second foot but millimeters away from gashed earth socket

Is not soul yelp

Is not spirit gouge

Is not ghost float

Is not shade drift

Is not quintessence slip

Is not fentanyl

Is not tramadol

Is not hydrocodone

Is not cooked rock

Is not analgesic ladder's final step off which unction follows flesh

Is not *fidelium defunctorum requiescant in pace*

Is not water pistol

Is not bitten-it coffin rot, rawhide, leather, paper, goo, gelatin, eye glue,
     crud, sludge, gunk melted into grease-trap like dumped soup scum
     into plastic garbage sack

Is not bought farm hairless hag hematoma-blackened-bruised, sputum
     producer in bed sag like disemboweled lung, wig slipped off pillow
     like a pug, nowhere hot, discarded by the babies like a broken
     string puppet

Is not scattered quintessence wind-wafted like exfoliated particles into
     quivering nostrils to be reincarnated as rat whisker

Is not petroleum flame in Pasadena, Texas, snapping off back of
     dashing psychopath collapsing to knees to face to ash, the liberated
     and relieved decent people turning to mowers and spacious kitch-
     ens clean as baby's toothless gums

Is not decapitation by car smash, Highway 116

Is not sudden infant crib husk

Is not the bowel-liquefying stomach-putrefying liver-atrophying patho-
     gens rushed into caged primates like a trillion mixer blades blend-
     ing precious guts

Is not after-fact, DOA, grit between molars, kicked bucket hillside
     tumble, doornail floor-plink, warmed over rump roast, limp-neck
     pheasant, coil uninhabited

is hauling up, exhausted, 250 lb. megalops on 50 lb. monofilament test
        secured with the 6-twist San Diego Jam Game-knot to carbon-steel
        circle-hook baited with one furious jack-rash and played with Daiwa
        Slatiga Lever Drag wrenched onto 8 ft. fiberglass stout, hauling up
        venerable heaving god, murderous, blood-zinging, monomaniacal,
        triumphant
is also love.

*T*O MAINTAIN HER approval I fake fearlessness.
I act indifferent to intractable death.
I offer rock-solidity.
I lie.
I always lie.
I mimic her exuberance
To reinforce her choice of mate.
I lie because I fear ridicule, dismissal.
I appear amazed by rhododendron.
I gush at oriole.
I pretend death does not ruin experience.
I feign positivism.
In this charade I reinforce her love,
While perfecting virtuosity.
So masterful at times I confound myself.
Personalities, like eyes, cross.
I have recaptured, I profess, childhood concentration,
Monolithic unselfconscious absorption
In the moment.
Amazingly, I have resurrected child.
I pulse this like blood
Cementing respect.
Imperative to lie for veracity
Would expose cowardice,
Petrification,
Amorphousness.
I agree that mortality's compression is
The wellspring of bliss.
I glow in this bogus philosophy.
Lying is the hospital in which I grow.
I offer her dependability
But to a close friend disclose wretchedness
Who registers same.

Old is shit, I tell him.

I panic, bark "no" into the dark.

Apropos nothing, I confess, I weep.

Suddenly crushing tears en route to Price Chopper.

Likewise, he says.

Parroting spirituality I adopt

The principles

Of the marveling personality.

So demoralized, I admit,

I fantasize suicide—

Carbon monoxide.

I alarm him

Who studies my face,

Clasps shoulder,

Exclaims I am beautiful, unique, irreplaceable,

That he, for one, would miss me, unutterably.

I secure from wife through practiced artfulness

The heartfelt outpouring

This friend delivers.

Perhaps even to him I lie.

(*I* **DANCE INSIDE** an open box to silver tinkling music.
I pirouette in netted tulle on my finely-silvered mirror.
The world seems draped of crystal thread, I quiver
Like a princess. I'm sprinkled with fragile ice-blue
Sequins down to ballet slippers—all aglitter spinning—
And shatter into chilled fire upon my brilliant image.)

*I*N THE FINAL episode he expires of overplus.
He's tuckered.
Life was pornographic gastronomic debauchery.
Women and tables, tables, women.
Illimitable succulence.
Boatloads of liver, head cheese, kidney, knuckle,
The vintner's magnificence.
Stripped mutton leg like Henry VIII, corn-holed queens.
Masturbated Venuses.
Caro. Black Strap. Sorghum. Tupelo.
Mango and cunt juice cluttered his beard.
In the final tableau diabetes, gout, diarrhea, gallstones.
Vultures attend.
Peck eyes.
String gut.
Dip blood.
Flock to bed.
Bawdy dissolution masticating meat while fingering wench under
        greasy boards.
Reaming hole till she yelps.
Humping again.
Hammering wedge of heavy cream, butter, sugar, dough.
Penis-eye spies a bitch, he charms her with brows.
Sucks her cunt like a half shell in ketchup.
Chases with Reddi Wip.
Rib-eye and Poupon, porkpie and kraut, sweetmeats and giblet.
Seborrheic Keratosis. Genital lesions. Horned toenails. Plaque.
Sixth wife heart-burst while bathing in come.
At the denouement hoary protagonist grunts
La Marseillaise,
Penis stuck inside like shriveled glove finger.
Vultures crowd headboard.
Something violent happens: life instantly flashes. Conquered prey.

Steaming gore. Intestine spill. Horny toes. Matted fur. Female rump. Mouth foam. Spermy towel. Waddling chin. Dowager stoop. Pianoforte. Ratty sock. Euphoria. Dopamine. Immortality. Mirror-kiss. Testosterone tub. Decomposition. Muscle-pump. Python flesh. Receding gum. Amnesia pudding. Tired pubis. Rocky bowel. Rubber tube. Astronaut umbilicus. Snapping flag. Candlewick smoke. Pasty thighs. Head-over-heel. Yellow callous. Cracked lake bed. Necrosis. Pall.

In the grand finale neither cranberry boar loin nor "Shugy Shugy Boom Boom" interest hero who grunts amidst scavengers his final word: fuck.

*Y*ESTERDAY **I** strolled with my friend's dead mother. She revealed family secrets: son's suicide, extramarital affair, self-incriminating diaries. She was tan, sturdy, breezily clad. Arm-in-arm we walked. Dusk fell. She smelled like spices. We spoke like adults on sobering topics of eternal significance. We parted as confidantes.

That afternoon I proved to Marcella her dead mother lives. (She suspected diaries, her mother paid for that transgression—daddy abandoned. Lou shot himself.) How came I to locked family secrets? Yes, she has a birthmark behind her left ear. "Uncanny," she declared.

I rushed to tell my wife news that death is not final, that personality survives, but she was riveted sheet metal with grommet head eyes. Her lips steel rectangles. I shook her, she rattled like junk sculpture. I wanted to recreate us with the simple phrase, "I am no longer ruined. I can breathe, I can love." But she was spot-welded, anodized, unbending. And I was expelled but with the resurrecting promise that world is magnificent, that breath is indemnification, and that death is a lie.

# GOODBYE GORDON.

Goodbye toes whose undersides I stroke like women's throats.

Goodbye castle gate guardsmen-fingers broadax-equipped conversant
on the subject of beheadings, betrayal, duplicity, gore.

Goodbye adamantine insistent thumbs clamping fingers into fist like
the battlefield oath before God and country to croak before
capitulation.

Goodbye buttocks on whose pachyderm I sit like a manifold mahout
across tangerine forests, butternut skies.

Goodbye ears whose every encroachment is an actionable offense.

Goodbye dependable peepers which got me through the lunatic wig-
wams of insufferable civilization into the primitive genitals of
princesses and sluts.

Goodbye practicable elbow chicken-skin pocked with the dictionary
of antediluvian grit and unendurable wit, and rubbed like indeci-
pherable braille by blind fingertips of chair arm, breakfast table,
park bench, tub.

Goodbye bulging latissimus dorsi dangerous as destroyers cleaving
brine, sculptural dependable wordless wings whose riveted sides
plow through seas of hypocrisy, ruthlessness, cruelty greed.

Goodbye in-curved sensual lips counterpart to nipple.

Goodbye baby Babinski foot toughened to cured animal-shod bone,
great knob of heel like redwood burl and cable bridge arc span-
ning cloud forest chasm, indenting the ground on which I trod
toward Zeus's thrust and anger and jealousy and vengeance and
lust.

Goodbye, finally, Gordon.

Goodbye imprisoning torturous rituals, embedded brain razors slicing
the gluey nerve-ball of me to stinging exposure and sandpa-
per-flay of irrational behavior, abandoned by God and remanded
to pitiful impotent psychological resistance.

Goodbye grandeur's pathetic delusion which projects me onto Sinai
as abducted patriarchal authoritarian talent intimidating to the

scribblers in the trough between mountains reeking of cowardice, copulation, trinkets, liquor.

Goodbye to insipidity of ego, pretentions and inaccuracies, posturing, preciousness, ingenious eccentricities intended to impress—self-flattery—goodbye to unmoored whole preposterous personality.

Goodbye to seizure.

Goodbye to failure.

Goodbye to brilliance.

Goodbye to ribcage of indecipherable cryptology.

Goodbye to tenacity.

Goodbye to passion.

Goodbye to testamentary will.

Goodbye to seductive addictive behavior.

Goodbye to hyperextended lust.

Goodbye to yarmulke knee caps davening in pants like two barbiturates, respite they need from falling and scraping and failing to achieve appreciable salvation.

Goodbye to banging carapace shins on bedframe and breakfront, dented and nicked from lifetime of disoriented dizzying eves of crisis and bliss, I lay them down like historical records—husks—on this terminal cot after rude innumerable disillusioning blunts.

Goodbye to Davy Crockett-Jim Bowie pituitary and endocrine system leading me into verbal and physical combat against superior militias in desolate places of creativity and inadequacy where I encounter delusion, isolation, grandeur, despair.

Goodbye to concrete-hard cranial bell housing blossoming words like Shasta daisies out perennial garden of eye-ear-nose in a chaotic spherical primitive planter of warthog connections inevitably creating an impacted root-bound elephantine sphere balanced atop fragile ill-equipped shoulders and spindly embarrassed sissified legs.

Goodbye old boy, Gordon, goodbye, to

Character

Personality

Episode

Sensation

Perception

Imagination

Attachment

Usefulness

Passion

Conundrum

Pleasure

Ecstasy

Hunger

Need.

It's been terrifically enjoyable. I'll mourn my passing. If the dead weep, at
the risk of ruining my masculine reputation, interminably I will.

*L*ET THERE BE death and tons of it!

To scrape world's table for new hungry tummies.

Let there be military death, civilian death.

Let there be death by attrition, death by geometrics.

Let there be battlefield massacre, metropolis bombing.

Let there be pandemic, epidemic, unspeakable terror.

Let there be parachutist, parafoil, ice climber failure.

Let there be race car flip, flame, crush-driver reprisal.

Let there be cholera, Ebola, bubonic disaster.

Let there be riots, aggression, murder, blood Sabbath.

Let there be births and loads of it!

Let there be twins, triplets, quadruplets, quintuplets.

Birth in bean field.

Birth in casino.

Birth in grandmother's rickety rocker.

Birth in subway and junked Ford Aerostar.

Birth in flame-thrower war-blackened horror.

Birth in classroom.

Birth on ferry.

Birth in theater.

Birth in grain elevator.

Birth in Papa Ginos.

Birth in barn attic.

Birth in bomb silo.

And birth in rusted cattery.

Let babies fill windows of Saint Mary's Episcopal.

Let there be millions upon millions of gasping depleted tits.

And millions upon millions of blistered insistent lips.

Let there be death by yard, acre, mile, sheet upon sheet of flat human
    corpses, unrolled like a bolt of milliner material.

Go all in: let there be The Millennium involving chasms spewing
    plasma; pythons vomiting fire; trees blooming tumors; sword
    protruding horses, rat infestation; excremental hamburger, the

botulism disease.

Let there be bankruptcy, bridges over rocky gorges.

(Publicly all will commiserate but privately savor others' tragedy.)

Let there be science fiction robots vaporizing screamers from television
screen heads.

Let there be tsunami, breach, flood, wash-out.

Bless mudslide, volcanic cloud slaughter.

Bless corpses like molecules roaring over fall to make way for the arrival
of fresh sass and brilliance.

Let there be sour breath, living flesh rot.

Let there be cranial soft spot, plantar clasp reflex.

Praise blender pureeing corpses.

Let there be monoxide suffocated blood.

Hail derelict hurled into mud.

Let there be termite infested scrotum and clogged fallopian head.

I am professorial psychopath randomly throttling coeds.

See me rotate on spit virgin and mother and witch.

Thank God for me, preserver of balance and order.

Savior with pusher and razor.

Who resists shall be stew, what obstructs shall be pie.

Let there be babies like LSD trips, birches leafing babies, every birch in
leaf, eight bawling fingertips with furious baby lips, cooing pop
bubbles and babbling astronauts, blowing burbling seed-heads and
gurgling nipplewort, babies departing thunderheads like a hard
green pea hail, slanting down air, shifting in wind, sheeting off
eaves, in mud gutter bursting diapered, sound, and powdered,

And for each one somewhere a corresponding demise.

*B*ITE MY BUTT, I say to Death.
Jump up ass.
Long walk, short pier.
Flying leap.
Fuck yourself.
Piss off.

Death grins. "My good man," it replies, "actuarial charts virtually insure your
demise within ten years, and given your medical history and dietary pre-
dilection—cake, ice cream, fried fat, sauce—indubitably either cardiac
event or stroke will kill you. I predict decomposition within seven, plus
or minus—extinction's not a precise calculation—and anticipate upon
your flesh an earth worm revival." Respectfully, Death rests its case.

Eat shit, I say.
Blow it out.
Cram it.
Play in street.

"Beg to differ," Death retorts, "reputation, not to mention livelihood, of our
actuarial geniuses depends on mathematical accuracy. You are poster
child—sixty-five, societally useless, "pastured", as they say, full of
exhausted possibilities. Yes, I'd love dolmades. Have you champagne?
Who knows, maybe renal failure or brain cancer. From sixty-five to
demise every year weighs like ten. I agree, hopeful man, a slit exists
through which you might slip. For every rule, exception. But don't
celebrate as fait accompli, it's more likely Sayonara."

Buzz off, I bark.
Fly a kite.
Eat dick
Jump in lake.

"*Au contraire,* it's for you *le petit mort finale.* Your patient paramour
    awaits, supine on fleece, Lethe-perfumed cleft, irresistible naked
    calix waving frankincense—unimaginable gift—and you acceler-
    ating toward her lips. Indeed, I can imagine—estranged, terrified,
    impotent—alcohol and barbiturates in a Motel 6, hastening the hour.
    Or blowing head off brain stem. Thank you, I would love the Chick-
    en Kiev or maybe, yes, the baked raspberry brie! My esteemed
    interlocutor, I mean no disrespect, but your hour approaches like a
    shadow edge. Truth is often awful and intrusive.

Fuck you, I rejoin.
Get lost.
Suck egg.
Beat retreat.
(I flick wrist as if dismissing pest.)
(I brush sleeve as if scattering dust.)
Piece of dung.
Pissant.
Bull shitter.
Horse ass.
Monkey rump.
(I grind heel as if crushing bug.)
And walk on, walk on to the beauty salon.

## I.

**S**KIPPING UPHILL to Daisy's house with
Courtship bouquet of roses, calamity
Donald tripped on twig, tumbled
And rolled web-over-bill and, cracking
Skull on boulder, lay dead amidst
A splatter of irrelevant petals.

## II.

Performing the power line tightrope routine
*En route* to liberate Tweetie, bib tied round
Neck, fork strapped to back, grin dripping
Yellow birdies, that fateful refrain batters
Feline's brain: Puddy Tat! Puddy Tat! Puddy
Tat! the instant before the electrical
Surge smokes his bones into words: "Eat
At Joes," "Eat At Joes," "Eat At Joes".

## III.

Boarded the jet to Malibu *en route* to Mickey
After years of equivocation, abandoning her
Life as the fashion guru, strapped in, tray
Upright, blanket on lap, Minnie's craft shook,
Boomed, spiraled down sky, and crashing
Through tube, exploded into flame
Gruesomely greasing the passengers.

STRANGLE MARKS on woman's neck
blackened arms of punished child
blown off hip of infantryman
carved out heart of sacrificial goat
burst from house child ablaze
terrified cowering cat
boy smoldering under father's fist
employee's anguish after colleague's betrayal
honor-suicide of the raped adolescent
blistering flesh of napalmed toddler
decapitated head of insurrectionist
trusting face of bolt-gunned cow
snap in half word-stick "forever"
vermin people hanged from lampposts
infant's guts on fascist's coat
lizard singed under magnifying glass
toad impaled to earth by shaft
thank you for haircut
into pincers slides Darwinian ant
rejection blunts artist's heart
draftee spilling bowel
surgeon crumpled at mugger's gun blast
bully strips sissy's books
insidious lies anesthetize public
life's work trashed by squeamish critics
condemning prisoner prosecution destroys exculpatory letter
hypocrite blunts accusing inner finger
licentious cop busts prostitute ring
at Rattlesnake Roundup dead prize-winning rattler
with pillowcase of oranges boss flogs cheater
after donkey dismounts horse the impotent mule
adolescents self-mutilate during Escape from Pain Week
Frodo Baggins, Samwise Gamgee under bridge sharing needle

master dumps Duchess on backwater highway

angel accepts candy from encompassing shadow

superman chooses woman sliding into gash over man plummeting off trestle

instant before snatching cockapoo crocodile's brain sprays across culvert

terror triggers compulsion in unthreatening setting

paranoia condemns X to dereliction

nun scours with Borax student's skepticism

bastard deposited on church's wet steps

bonehead floods romantic's uterus in which occurs tragedy

bloated hogs litter field after God's white phosphorous

barbecues bogies the happy bomber under Jesus' blessing-blister

background mother's starving palms beseeching worker at food truck

dead Muslim's wailing father

nation stunned after assassination

child's descent into schizophrenia

soldier bashes baby against wall; mother crumples

castigated boy torturing lizard

the frustrated thrashing the child who murders the sparrow

rattler of memory striking rat of terror

parade of heroes parting sticky buffoons

clipping heart with disingenuous scissors

television bleaching brain with Clorox

institution car-crushing originality

dejection shaped like a human body

crucifix, star, crescent and other materiel

white of joy surrounding yolk of rage

*"Insulated romantic love was insufficient, larger forces dominated—imperfection, anger, OCD—especially that monstrous despotic Nazi OCD torturing me like a helpless worm—I lost all power, it finally broke me. Don't blame yourself. Lovers, you know, cannot remake each other. Nobody's responsible. I always loved you. I'm sorry, profoundly. Please forgive this horrible selfishness."*

*I*'M FRESHLY DECEASED. My wife doesn't know.

I'm crumpled on floor against a kitchen cabinet.

Collapsed like a puppet, shelved, unimportant.

Heart attack.

Lipitor failed.

Clutched chest, groaned. Death foreshortened suffering.

Couldn't break my descent.

Mercifully, dirt blinds my parents.

Sister will be shocked,

Wife devastated.

Don't let it be she who discovers me.

What could be crueler?

But how am I praying? I'm theoretical.

If I could but crawl to bed to appear less unnatural.

Soon, she'll return and in horror decry me.

Incredibly, my friend discovered his dead wife.

Torpedoed his resolve. Overnight white.

Can't bar the door—objects pass through me.

Can't intervene. Am fearful for her.

I look like a stupid film noir victim.

She has arrived,

Atmospheric disruptions.

Dog collar jangle.

Turn back, I scream.

She disabuses package, goes to toilet.

Steps away my mess awaits.

Can't even close eyelids.

She bought ice cream, Peanut Butter Cup!

Between the functional and ruined lies the abyss.

Makes ice cream seem comical.

Now water flushes.

Now dog nails clatter.

Now she passes mudroom, table, breakfront, island.

She's near, perplexed by my absence.
Terror grips.
I cannot prevent collision.

*M*Y BOUNDLESS STOMACH. Into her I shovel rasher, rib, lobster,
pheasant, hamburger, national flag, Minnesotan lake, library,
estuaries of women, condominium, vacation liner, beet
plantation, ballet, bomb, cake icing, blueberry compote,
Caro pie, paradise square, Ben and Jerry's repertoire,
hot caramel, immortality, death, war-slaughter, Picasso,
Dali, Bach suites, disembodied vagina, stained teeth,
oleomargarine thigh, long neck toes, black toenail,
cardiac infarction, thyroid cancer, brain cancer, penis
canker, The David, Battleship Oklahoma, rattlesnake
steak, megalomania, totalitarianism, genocide, dog
claw, Herman Melville, belly dancer, Thailand whore,
Jesus Nazareth, Satan, bone-in, raw oyster, muscles,
humpback whale, human embryo, foie gras, my dead
parents, Richthofen's tri-plane, Eydie Gorme, terror,
trepidation, starry island, root system, branches,
test tube, blood taint, syphilis, religious purity, high
notes, intolerance, racism, anti-Semitism, broken
treaty, Mahatma Gandhi, skull pyramid, my fingers,
knees, feet, I suck myself off, I massage myself, I
slurp ladle of semen, I suck honeycomb vulva, my
lips impregnate, I split thighs like crumble cake, I
masturbate siren, I eat lover's shit, I teeth-rip wrist
onto lavender plate, spit veins, I eat fame, vermicelli,
suicide, tomato clam, rusted wrench, Earth's liquid
center, smelter of lead, basketball stadium, money,
I eat money, money pulled from cunt, ejaculated
through shaft, extracted from ear, corpse money,
fuck money, frag money, hacked through human
sternum money, I pull money from throat like heavy
clothesline, nose-rubbed-in-piss money, I vomit
nail, ankle, fibula, heart valve, I vomit immemorial
sculpture, I vomit kitchen utensil, I vomit clean tack

and vaginal lube, I vomit venereal infection, crabs, I
vomit and re-slurp biblical leprosy, I eat hair-lip,
obesity, I eat flatulence, I drink halo and ostrich plume, I
slam bathtub full of fraternity fuck-punch, I suck down
sour mash distillery, and weave into bishops, I eat bishop
penis, I cream bishopric like rhesus, I lick Reddi Wip
off human brain, girlfriend's brain red-veined, I dump
in gullet jarred maraschino and intelligence, I tooth-
scrape baked politics off shank, ink off cartridge, guano
off pier, I eat cat litter, I ketchup iguana scale, death-
fear, death-terror, death-wish, death-catechism with
Worcestershire Prayer, John Baptist's hair, I'm bisexual
and eat razor blade, I'm trisexual and eat tenth estate,
I wear my mother's areola like beret, I tilt banquet
table into mouth stretched round end like a garbage
pail, I eat narcissism dumpling pale as fish tummy, don't
care what you think of this, if you're sick quit fucking
reading, I eat you, too, your disgust, sanctimonious-
ness, squeamishness, I eat your critical ignorance,
this is not poetry, I'm no poet, I'm your savage, jackal,
cannibal, I eat your meticulousness and predetermined
failure, my gut pulses with my own scrotum like dazzling
sun under midriff, beware my lovelies, my life's a
digestive track breaking into component bits flashes
of star-blast, everything actual and fantastical.

# EPILOGUE

EPILOGUE

*T*HERE'S NOTHING more to say.
Nothing.
Finally, I am spent.
Dejection, despair.
Numb.
I'm saying nothing now.
Merely disclosing the cadaverous message of incapacity.
Skull an empty carapace.
I continue in emptiness
To say I failed youth's romantic fantasy of heroism,
My Zarathustrian destiny.
Scorpion with cracked thorax crawling sideways.
The poet possesses innumerable images
With which to say nothing:
Scorpion, crab, centipede, deliquescence.
I leave it to orators
In their legions
To continue insistent disquisition.
I leave it to warrior-artists.
Pity me not for I have attained status
Of profound stupidity,
In which absence of knowledge is a tribute,
Laurel laid upon one who has
Lost the torture of exactitude.
Bless you all your passionate conviction.

*Acknowledgments*


*Descant (Canada)*

*CV2 (Canada)*

*Drunken Boat*

*Court Green*

*Columbia Poetry Review*